EARLY BUSINESS CONTACTS

OTHER ESP TITLES OF INTEREST INCLUDE:

Brieger, N. and J. Comfort
*Advanced Business Contacts**
Brieger, N. and J. Comfort
*Developing Business Contacts**
Brieger, N. and A. Cornish
*Secretarial Contacts**
Brieger, N. and J. Comfort
*Technical Contacts**
Brieger, N. and J. Comfort
*Social Contacts**
Brieger, N. and J. Comfort
Business Issues
Brieger, N. and S. Sweeney
The Language of Business English
Davies, S. *et al.*
Bilingual Handbooks of Business Correspondence and Communication
Goddard, C.
*Business Idioms International**
McGovern, J. and J. McGovern
*Bank on Your English**
Palstra, R.
*Telephone English**
Pote, M. *et al.*
*A Case for Business English**

Business Management English Series:
Brieger, N, and J. Comfort
*Production and Operations**
Brieger, N. and J. Comfort
*Personnel**
Brieger, N. and J. Comfort
Language Reference for Business English
Comfort, J. and N. Brieger
*Marketing**
Comfort, J. and N. Brieger
*Finance**

*Includes audio cassette(s)

EARLY BUSINESS CONTACTS

Nick Brieger
and
Jeremy Comfort

Prentice Hall
New York London Toronto Sydney Singapore

PRENTICE HALL INTERNATIONAL ENGLISH LANGUAGE TEACHING

To Anna, Lisa and Daniel

First published 1994 by
Prentice Hall International (UK) Ltd
Campus 400, Maylands Avenue
Hemel Hempstead
Hertfordshire, HP2 7EZ
A division of Simon & Schuster International Group

© Prentice Hall International (UK) Ltd, 1994

All rights reserved. No part of this publication may be reproduced, stored in a retrieval system, or transmitted, in any form, or by any means, electronic, mechanical, photocopying, recording or otherwise, without prior permission, in writing, from the publisher.
For permission within the United States of America contact Prentice Hall Inc., Englewood Cliffs, NJ 07632

Illustrations by Mike Lacey, Harry Venning and Taurus Graphics
Designed by D & J Hunter
Typeset in Melior/Futura
Printed and bound in Spain by Mateu Cromo, S.A. Pinto (Madrid)

Library of Congress Cataloging-in-Publication Data

Brieger, Nick.
    Early business contacts / Nick Brieger and Jeremy Comfort.
       p. cm.
    1. English language--Business English. 2. English language--Textbooks for foreign speakers. 3. Business--Problems, exercises, etc. I. Comfort, Jeremy. II Title.
PE1115.B6834 1994
428.3' 4--dc20

                                                  93-43740
                                                     CIP

British Library Cataloguing in Publication Data

A catalogue record for this book is available from the British Library

ISBN   0-13-042540-0

1 2 3 4 5 98 97 96 95 94

Contents

Introduction		1
To the Student		3
To the Teacher		5

The contents list below indicates the topic themes for each unit on the left, followed by the language area or communication skill.

Unit 1	First meetings 1 (*Introductions and greetings*)	7
Unit 2	First meetings 2 (*Presenting yourself*)	11
Unit 3	First contact (*Social English 1*)	15
Unit 4	Further contact (*Social English 2*)	20
Unit 5	Company organisation (*Presenting the company*)	25
Unit 6	Supply (*Describing product features*)	30
Unit 7	Making arrangements (*Telephoning*)	35
Unit 8	Information handling (*Checking and confirming*)	39
Unit 9	Job routines (*Present simple & expressions of frequency*)	45
Unit 10	Current projects (*Present continuous*)	50
Unit 11	Business correspondence (*Letter writing*)	55
Unit 12	Sales review (*Describing graphs*)	63
Unit 13	Sales forecasts (*Intentions and predictions*)	68
Unit 14	Company results (*Present perfect v. past simple*)	72
Unit 15	Company strategy (*Conditional 1*)	76
Unit 16	Competition (*Comparison of adjectives*)	79
Unit 17	Project timing (*Prepositions of time*)	83
Unit 18	Factory tour (*Prepositions of place*)	87
Unit 19	Market research (*Question formation*)	91
Unit 20	The budget meeting (*Modals*)	95
	Key Section (Units 1 – 20)	99
	Glossary	139
	Appendix	154

Introduction

TARGETS AND OBJECTIVES

This book is aimed at students who have a professional need for Business English; people either in, or training for, jobs in the business world.

More specifically, the material is relevant for learners, at pre-intermediate level or above, who need revision or further practice in developing listening skills for:

- extracting relevant information
- structuring information
- inferring meaning from context
- becoming accustomed to different varieties of English.

The material also develops speaking skills through:

- problem-solving activities
- role-plays
- discussion topics.

ORGANISATION OF MATERIAL

There are 20 units in the first part of the book (see Contents page). Each unit consists of:

1. LISTENING

A taped listening passage, accompanied by an information task.

2. PRESENTATION

Language items from the listening passage highlighted and explained.

3. CONTROLLED PRACTICE

Exercises designed to give practice in the language items introduced in the Presentation.

4. TRANSFER

Pair work, or occasionally group work, designed to encourage students to use the language introduced and to practise it in a freer context.

WORD CHECK

A glossary of the business vocabulary that appears in the listening passage.

KEY SECTION

The second part of the book contains the Key section for each unit. This includes:

1. LISTENING

A tapescript and answers to the listening task.

2. CONTROLLED PRACTICE	Answers to the controlled-practice exercises.
3. TRANSFER (where necessary)	Information for pair-work activities.
GLOSSARY	At the end of the book there is a glossary of frequently used business terms.
APPENDIX	After the glossary there is an appendix of common irregular verbs.
THE ROLES OF TEACHER AND STUDENT	The materials provide the teacher with an opportunity to strike a balance between two classroom roles: teacher-controlled and teacher-monitored. They also give students an opportunity for autonomous learning (self-study).
	Sections 1. **Listening**, 2. **Presentation**, 3. **Controlled Practice**, and the **Word Check** section can be worked through with or without a teacher. Section 4. **Transfer** can be worked through by students in pairs or groups without a teacher, but some form of teacher monitoring is advisable.

To the Student

WHO IS EARLY BUSINESS CONTACTS FOR?

This material is for students who have some previous knowledge of English and wish to apply it in a business context. It can be used by students working alone, as self-study or homework material during a business course, or as follow-up material after a business course.

SELECTION OF MATERIAL

You can work through the material starting at Unit 1. Alternatively, you can choose units on the basis of the topic or the language area or skill covered (see Contents page).

USING A UNIT

All of the units can be done without a teacher. All the sections in a unit can also be done without a teacher except for the Transfer activities (but see below).

1. LISTENING

This tells you something about the unit. All the listening activities have an exercise with them.

- Read through the introduction to the Listening section. Make sure you understand what you have to do while you are listening.
- Play the tape right through without stopping.
- As you listen, try to do the exercise.
- If necessary, listen to the tape again. Stop the tape and replay sections if you need to.
- Check your answers with the Key at the back of the book.
- If your answers are wrong, listen again. You can check the tapescript in the Key. Use the Word Check if you cannot understand some of the words.

2. PRESENTATION

- Read carefully through the presentation and explanation of the language area.
- Try to remember how this language was used on the tape. If you wish, listen to the tape again.

3. CONTROLLED PRACTICE

- Complete the exercises.
- Check your answers with the Key.
- If your answers are wrong, look again at the Presentation, and try to see why you have made mistakes.

Note: We have used the following symbols. They show you what is missing in the exercises:

.... one or more words ———— only one word.

4. TRANSFER These activities involve speaking. You can do the pair-work speaking activities without a teacher. However, these activities are best done with a teacher who can correct your spoken language.

If you do the pair-work speaking activities with a colleague, follow this procedure:

- Decide who is Student A and who is Student B.
- Student A should look *only* at the Student A copy.
- Student B should look *only* at the Student B copy in the Key section.
- Carry out the Transfer activity. Try to use the language you have learnt.

WORD CHECK The words are taken from the listening passages. Try to think how you could use these words yourself.

To the Teacher

USES OF THE MATERIAL
- As a complete course for students of Business English.
- As supplementary material to a general English course for students with an interest in or a need for Business English.
- As a self-study/homework component of a Business English course.
- As follow-up material on completion of a Business English course.

SELECTION OF MATERIAL

The units are not graded. Teachers may, therefore, select according to:

- Topic (see Contents page)
- Language area/skill (see Contents page).

USING A UNIT
1. LISTENING

At the beginning of each unit there is a short introduction to the topic. The input text for each unit is a listening passage.

- Prepare the students for the task. Make sure they are absolutely clear what they have to do.
- Play the tape right through, without stopping.
- For many students it will be necessary to give them an opportunity to listen to the tape again. Replay the tape, stopping at appropriate places.
- Let the students check their answers with the Key.
- Play the tape again if there are major differences between the Key and the students' answers.
- Refer the students to the Word Check if there are vocabulary problems.

2. PRESENTATION
- Ask the students to read through the Presentation and explanation of the language area.
- Get them to give you additional examples of the language presented.
- If necessary, look at the tapescript in the Key to identify examples of the language.

3. CONTROLLED PRACTICE
- Ask the students to complete the exercises and then check their answers with the Key.
- Advise on alternative answers or give more practice where necessary.

Note: The following symbols have been used to indicate what is missing in the exercises:

.... one or more words   _____ only one word.

4. TRANSFER

These activities involve speaking – mostly pair work.

- Divide the class into pairs.
- Assign roles (Student A and Student B). Make sure they only look at their own role/information (Student B's information is always in the Key section).
- Monitor the pairs while they carry out the speaking transfer, prompting the use of practised language if necessary.

WORD CHECK

The words are taken from the listening passages. The glossary only provides definitions. This section can be used before, during or after the listening activity.

Unit 1

First meetings 1

Introductions and greetings

1. LISTENING You are going to hear a number of people introducing themselves. Some of the introductions involve two people, some involve three. First look at the conversations in the pictures below. Then, as you listen, number these conversations in the order you hear them. The first one has been done for you.

2. Presentation

Introductions often include these steps:

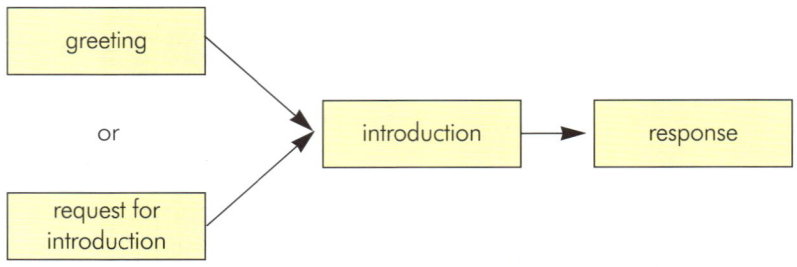

You heard two types of introduction:
- introducing yourself
- introducing someone else

2.1 Introducing yourself

Greeting	Introduction	Response
Hello	Let me introduce myself. My name's _____	Pleased to meet you. I'm _____
Good morning/ afternoon	My name's _____	Nice to meet you. Mine's _____
How do you do?	I'm _____	Nice to meet you. I'm ___

— 8 —

2.2 Introducing someone else

Request for introduction	Introduction	Response
Could you introduce me to _____?	Of course. Let me introduce you to _____	Nice to meet you.
I haven't met _____	I'm sorry. This is _____	Very nice to meet you.
I don't know anyone here. You'll have to introduce me.	Of course. I'll introduce you to _____, this is _____	Nice to meet you.
	Let me introduce you two. _____, this is _____	Nice to meet you.

Notes:
1. Some introductions are more formal than others. The use of first names indicates *informality*.
2. In English-speaking cultures, people usually *shake hands* on first meeting.

Now listen again and indicate whether the introduction is *formal* (F) or *informal* (I). The first one has been done for you.

Introduction 1 (*F*)   Introduction 5 ( )

Introduction 2 ( )   Introduction 6 ( )

Introduction 3 ( )   Introduction 7 ( )

Introduction 4 ( )

3. CONTROLLED PRACTICE

Complete the introductions.

1. Peter King introduces himself to Jack Simpson:

   Peter King: Hello, ... My name's Peter King.

   Jack Simpson: .... I'm Jack Simpson.

2. Philip introduces Sarah to James:

   Sarah: Philip, I .... here. You'll have to ....

   Philip: Of _____, I'll .... to James. He's an old friend of mine.

   James, ... Sarah, she's just joined the company.

   James: ...., Sarah. Where do you come from?

3. Rod Burton introduces Pete Taylor to an important customer:

   Pete: Rod, I .... Mrs Rogers, the Purchasing Manager from Kentons.

   Rod: I'm _____. Come and meet her. Mrs Rogers,

   .... Pete Taylor, our Export Sales Manager.

   Mrs Rogers: .... What countries do you cover?

4. Klaus Fischer introduces himself to an American visitor:

   Klaus Fischer: How .... ? My ....

   American: .... _____ Brenda Cole.

4. Transfer

Group work
Work in groups of three.

1. Introduce yourself to the others.
2. Introduce the other two to each other.
3. Ask to be introduced.

WORD CHECK

Marketing Manager	person in charge of the marketing department
Computer Manager	person in charge of the computer department
yet	up to now (in questions and negatives)
to be over	to be here on a visit from another country
host	person who invites or receives guests
to move	to go to live in a new house/town/area
these parts	this area

Unit 2

First meetings 2

Presenting yourself

1. LISTENING Manders Plc are having their annual party. Listen to the dialogues overheard at the party. Match up the people's names with their type of work. The first one has been done for you.

Names	Type of work
1. Peter	a. Production
2. John	b. Personal Assistant
3. Susan	c. software development
4. Mike	d. market research
5. Sarah	e. fashion design
6. Mr Fields	f. Personnel
7. Martin	g. Accounts
8. Jean	h. Sales
9. Jean's husband	i. Finance

(1 — Peter matches with c. software development)

2. PRESENTATION

It is very common to present yourself in terms of your job. The job identifies the person. The dialogues that you heard follow a certain pattern:

Question/Comment	Filler	Response	Comment/Question
A: What do you do (for a living)?	B: Well,	I'm in computers.	B: Not a bad job.
A: Do you work?		B: Yes, I'm a fashion designer.	A: That's interesting.
A: What do you do (in the _____ Department)?	B: Oh,	I'm on the market research side.	B: What about you?/ And you?
A: I haven't seen you around before.		B: No, I've just started with Manders. I'm in the Sales Department.	A: What do you do there?

Notes:
1. We often use the simple present when talking about jobs.
   e.g. A: What *do* you *do*?
   B: *I work* for Manders.
2. We use a variety of prepositions to indicate work relationships.
   e.g. I work *for* Manders (they are my employers)
   I work *at* Manders (the place)
   I work *with* Manders (a sense of collaboration)
   I'm *in* computers (general type of work)
   I'm *on* the market research side (general type of work)
   I'm *in* the Sales Department (specific place of work)

3. CONTROLLED PRACTICE

A. Complete the sentences with an appropriate preposition.

B. Choose the most appropriate response.

1. I'm in computers. What about you?
   a. Oh, I live in London.
   b. Well, I work in Sales.
   c. Oh, I've been here for years.

2. I'm Mr Jones' secretary. He's the Production Manager.
   a. Ah, that's interesting.
   b. Is that one of your colleagues over there?
   c. Oh, I haven't met him.

3. I live in Paris. What about you?
   a. I'm a fashion designer.
   b. I live right here.
   c. Well, I work from home.

4. My husband's in the Production Department.
   a. I'm in the Sales Department.
   b. Not a bad job.
   c. Oh yes, I think I've met him.

5. Hello, I'm Sarah. I haven't seen you around before.
   a. What do you do for a living?
   b. Is that one of your colleagues?
   c. No, I'm new here.

4. Transfer

Pair work
Student B: Turn to the Key section.
Student A: Use the business cards below to practise introductory conversations. Tell Student B about your job and place of work, and find out about Student B's occupation.

M O P roductions Plc
Sandy Vincent
Art Director
235 High Street London W6 7DP
Tel: 081 743 5892 Fax: 081 743 6351

I • N • F • O
• TEC •

Michelle Martine
Design Engineer

Rue Montoyer 419
1040 Brussels

Phone 2–513 8654
Fax 2–511 4987

TELECON Spa.

Franco Brunello
Export Sales Manager

23 via Roma, Torino, Italy
Tel: 11 669 4632
Fax: 11 657 2943

WORD CHECK

Plc	Public Limited Company. A company whose shares you can buy on the Stock Exchange
annual	every year, yearly
software	programs for a computer system
development	planning new products
Personnel Department	section of a company which deals with staff welfare, records, training and recruitment
colleague	fellow worker in a company or profession
Accounts Department	section of a company which deals with money paid or received
market research	examination of the possible demand for a product before it is put on the market
Personal Assistant	secretary who provides special help to a manager or director
Finance	section of a company which controls a company's money
Production Department	section of a company which deals with the making of the company's products
fashion designer	person who plans new styles in clothes

Unit 3

First contact

Social English 1

1. LISTENING When you meet someone for the first time and start up a conversation, it is important to find points of common interest so that the conversation can run smoothly. Listen to the five dialogues on the tape. Decide if you think they are successful (✔) or not (✘) in making initial contact.

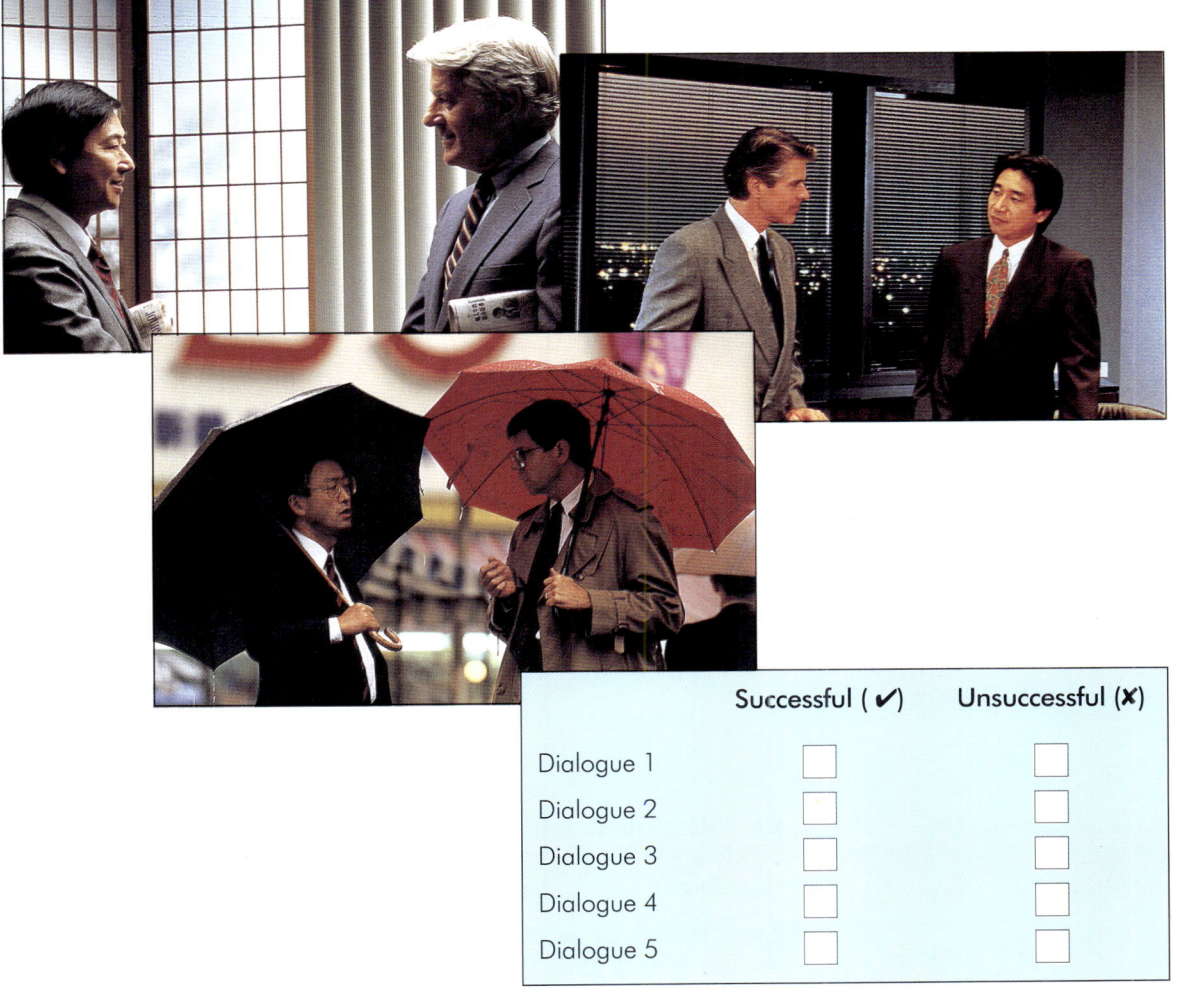

	Successful (✔)	Unsuccessful (✘)
Dialogue 1	☐	☐
Dialogue 2	☐	☐
Dialogue 3	☐	☐
Dialogue 4	☐	☐
Dialogue 5	☐	☐

Now listen again and note down the answers to these questions.

Dialogue 1:   Has the visitor been to Japan before? _____

Dialogue 2:   Which hotel is the visitor staying in? _____

Dialogue 3:   What topic of common interest do they find? _____

Dialogue 4:   What topic of common interest do they find? _____

Dialogue 5:   What topic of common interest do they find? _____

2. PRESENTATION

Successful conversation depends on finding a topic both people can easily talk about. One way of reaching this point is to follow a number of steps until a topic of common interest is found. A typical sequence might be:

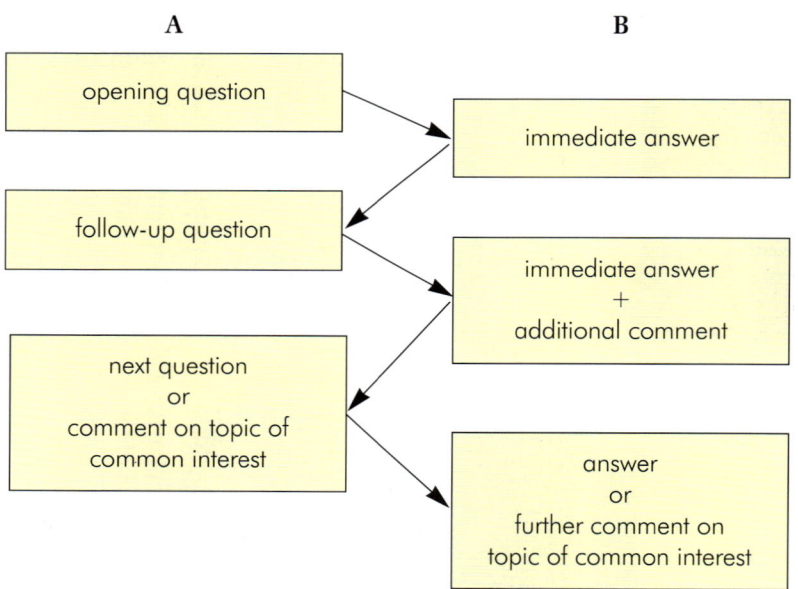

Now look more closely at the typical sequence of conversation.

2.1   Opening question
Is this your first trip to ....?
How was your trip?

2.2   Immediate answer
Yes, it is.
Fine, thanks.

2.3   Follow-up question
Are you staying long?
Business or pleasure?

2.4 Immediate answer
No.
Business.

Note: These answers are not helpful in finding a common interest. You need to make an additional comment.

2.5 Additional comment
But hopefully not my last.
Unfortunately only a couple of weeks.
Business, I'm afraid. My company is setting up an office here in Tokyo.

2.6 Next question
Have you found time to see much?
Really? Where is your company based?

2.7 Establishing topic of common interest
Are you interested in gardens?
Oh, I visited Detroit a couple of years ago.
That's a coincidence. My wife is in fashion, too.

3. CONTROLLED PRACTICE

The following four dialogues are in the wrong order. Rearrange them to make a natural flow of conversation.

Dialogue 1

	Really? What did you expect?
	No, I've been to the States before, but this is the first time in Atlanta.
	So, what do you think of Atlanta?
	Fine, I'll see what I can arrange.
	Well, it's not what I expected.
	There is a part like that. You must let me show you around.
	Well, I suppose I thought it would be more traditional.
	That would be interesting.
1	Is this your first trip over here?

Dialogue 2

	I'm sure. I hope to get back here again.
	That's a pity. There's a lot to see.
	Good. Are you here on business then?
	Are you staying long?

☐ Really? That's interesting. What line are you in?
☐ No, just a couple of days.
☐ Yes, we're thinking of setting up an office here.

Dialogue 3
☐ That would be nice.
☐ That's interesting. My son is an editor on the local paper.
☐ I believe you're in journalism.
☐ Really? I expect I'll meet him.
☐ Yes, that's right – on the editorial side.
☐ Yes, what about coming round for a drink? I could introduce you to him.

Dialogue 4
☐ Scotland. This time of year it's pretty cold.
☐ A bit warmer than back home.
☐ Well, if you do come across, you must visit us.
☐ Oh, so where do you come from?
☐ Yes, that's right. The best time to visit is in the summer.
☐ I can imagine. I've never been but people tell me it's very beautiful.
☐ How do you find the weather here?
☐ Maybe I'll get across next year.

4. Transfer

Pair work

Engage your partner in conversation. Try to establish a common interest.
e.g. a place, a hobby, a job, family, etc.

WORD CHECK

trip	journey away from home, e.g. to a foreign country
interesting	something which takes and keeps one's interest, e.g. Tokyo is an interesting city.
hopefully	I hope that ...
interested	having or showing interest, e.g. Are you interested in gardens?
hobby	free time activity
unfortunately	by bad luck
pleasure	enjoyment
to set up	to establish
to be based	to have one's headquarters
fashion	styles in clothes
design	planning and drawing
coincidence	surprising combination of events, happening by chance
to fix ... up	to arrange

Unit 4

Further contact

Social English 2

1. LISTENING   **A** Responding appropriately in social situations is an important part of communication. Below is an example of an appropriate and an inappropriate response.

Appropriate response

Inappropriate response

On the tape you will hear a number of responses. Decide whether the responses you hear are appropriate ✔ or not ✘. The first one has been done for you.

1. ✔   6. ☐   11. ☐
2. ☐   7. ☐   12. ☐
3. ☐   8. ☐   13. ☐
4. ☐   9. ☐   14. ☐
5. ☐ 10. ☐   15. ☐

B Now listen again. This time all the responses are appropriate.

2. PRESENTATION

Polite responses can be grouped into several categories. This section gives examples of different situations and tells you what you can say.

Situation	Response
Thanking Thanks for your help. Thanks for the lovely meal.	Not at all. You're welcome. Glad you liked/enjoyed it.
Apologising Sorry, I must have got the wrong number.	It doesn't matter Don't worry. Never mind.
Inviting Would you like to come to dinner? How about a drink?	Yes, I'd like/love to. That would be nice. That's a good idea.
Asking permission *If the answer is 'yes'* May I come in? Do you mind if I smoke? *If the answer is 'no'* Do you mind if I smoke?	Yes, of course. Please do. Certainly. No, of course not. No, not at all. Well, actually, I'd prefer you didn't/not to. I'd rather you didn't.
Giving news *Bad news* I didn't get that job. My father died last night. *Good news* We've had a fantastic year. *Surprising news* She's 99 years old, you know.	 Never mind. Better luck next time. Oh, I am sorry to hear that. I'm glad to hear that. Congratulations. Really?

Agreeing I think we should leave now. I hope it doesn't rain.	So do I. I hope so too. Me too.
Giving good wishes Have a good weekend.	You too. Same to you.

3. CONTROLLED PRACTICE

Write down an appropriate response. The first one has been done for you.

1. We lost the match.

   Never mind. Better luck next time.

2. Do you mind if I open the window?

   ....

3. Would you like to go to a concert this evening?

   ....

4. Sorry, I interrupted you.

   ....
   ....

5. Could you pass me the file?

   ....
   ....

6. I hope he gets the job.

   ....
   ....

7. Have a good Christmas.

....
....

8. She's only 22 and she's already head of the Sales Department.

....
....

9. I think it's going to rain.

....
....

10. Thanks. That was a delicious meal.

....
....

11. My car broke down again this morning.

....
....

12. Can I see you for a moment?

....
....

13. How about something to eat?

....
....

14. You must come round for dinner.

....
....

15. I'm sorry. I've taken the wrong file.

....
....

4. Transfer

Pair work

Student A: Look at the table in the Presentation section. For each situation listed (thanking, apologising, inviting etc.), make a statement.
e.g. (thanking) Thank you for helping me with this exercise.

Student B: Respond appropriately to Student A's statements.
e.g. You're welcome.

When you have finished, Student B make statements and Student A respond appropriately.

WORD CHECK

to respond	to reply
response	answer
appropriately	in the right way
lovely	enjoyable
glad	happy, pleased
to hand	to give
concert	musical performance

Unit 5

Company organisation

Presenting the company

1. LISTENING   Listen to the presentation about Rossomon Plc. As you listen, complete the organisation chart below.

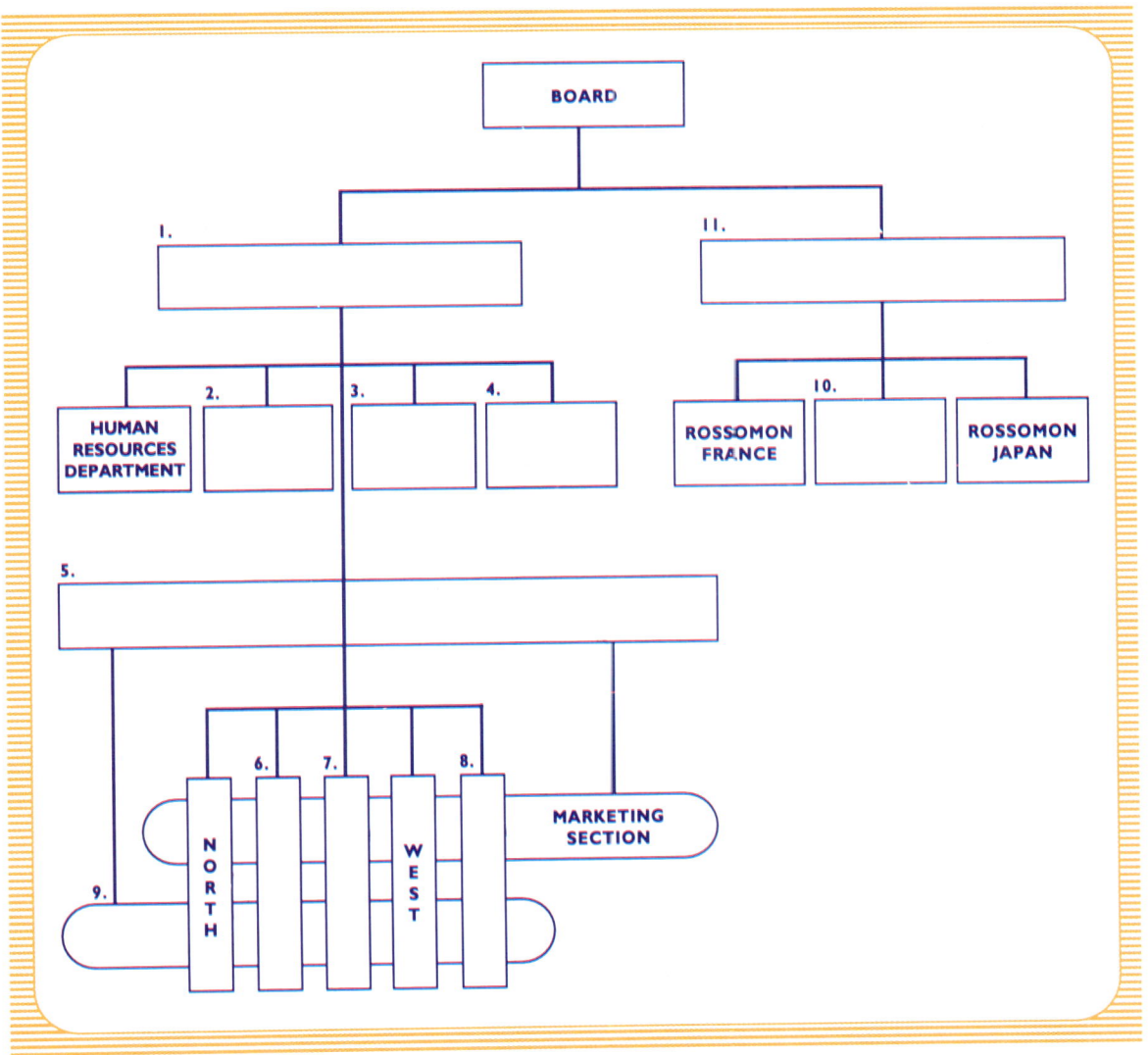

2. Presentation

This section demonstrates some of the language used to describe an organisation in terms of:

- hierarchy
- responsibilities/functions
- titles
- affiliates
- structure

2.1 Hierarchy

The company **is headed by** the MD.
The Sales Director **reports to** the MD.
The Sales Director **is under** the MD.
The Sales Director **is accountable to** the MD.
The Sales Director **is supported by** a sales team.
The Sales Director **is assisted by** an Assistant Sales Manager.

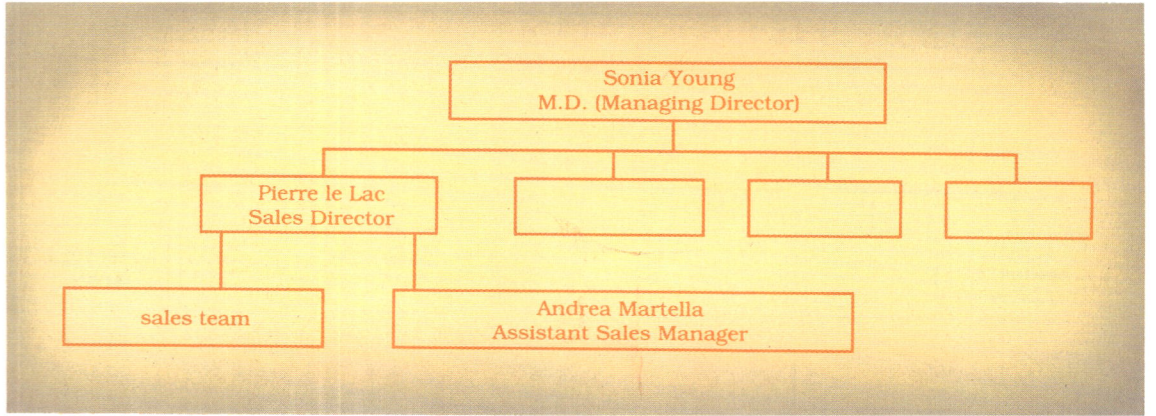

2.2 Responsibilities/functions

The Finance Department **is responsible for** accounting.
The R & D (Research and Development) Department **takes care of** new product development.
The Administration Manager **is in charge of** personnel.

2.3 Titles

Below are the main managerial titles with the US equivalents in brackets:
Chairman (President)
Managing Director (Chief Executive Officer/Senior Vice-President)
Finance Director (Vice-President – Finance)
Sales Manager (Sales Director)

Note: The Directors and Chairman of a company usually sit on the Board of Directors (Executive Board).

2.4 Affiliates

X is the **parent company**.
A, B and C are **subsidiaries** (more than 50% owned by the parent).

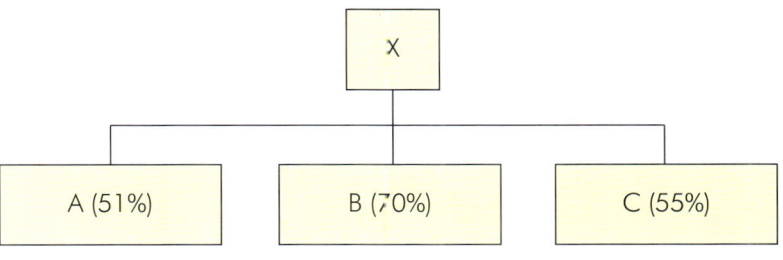

2.5 Structure

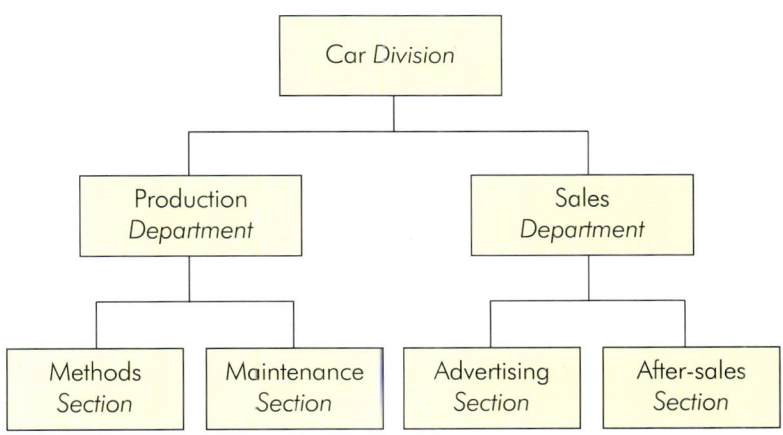

The Car Division **consists of** the Production Department and the Sales Department.
The Production Department **comprises** the Methods Section and the Maintenance Section.
The Sales Department **is made up of** the Advertising Section and the After-sales Section.

3. CONTROLLED PRACTICE

Use the organisation chart in the Listening section and the language in the Presentation section to complete these sentences.

1. The Managing Director .... to the Board.
2. The Managing Director .... for running the company.
3. The Managing Director .... by four executive departments.
4. _____ the Managing Director, there are five regional divisions.
5. Each Regional Manager .... of a territory.

6. The five regions .... by two other sections – Marketing and Technical Services.

7. The Section Leaders .... to the Regional Managers.

8. In addition to the ———————— company, Rossomon has three ————————————.

9. The subsidiaries .... Rossomon France, Rossomon Germany and Rossomon Japan.

10. The subsidiaries .... to the Export Sales Department.

4. Transfer

Pair work

Student B: Turn to the Key section.

Student A:

1. Describe the typical management structure of a British company to Student B. Use the organisation chart for Semling Photographics.

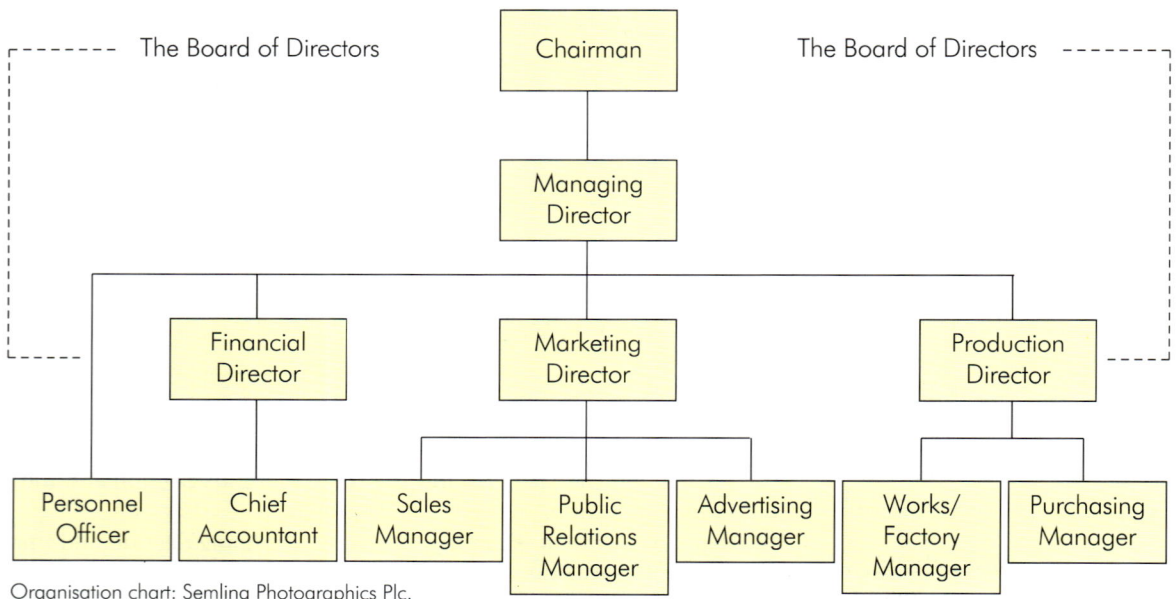

Organisation chart: Semling Photographics Plc.

2. Listen to Student B's description of the typical management structure of an American company. Use the information to complete the organisation chart for Felton Computers.

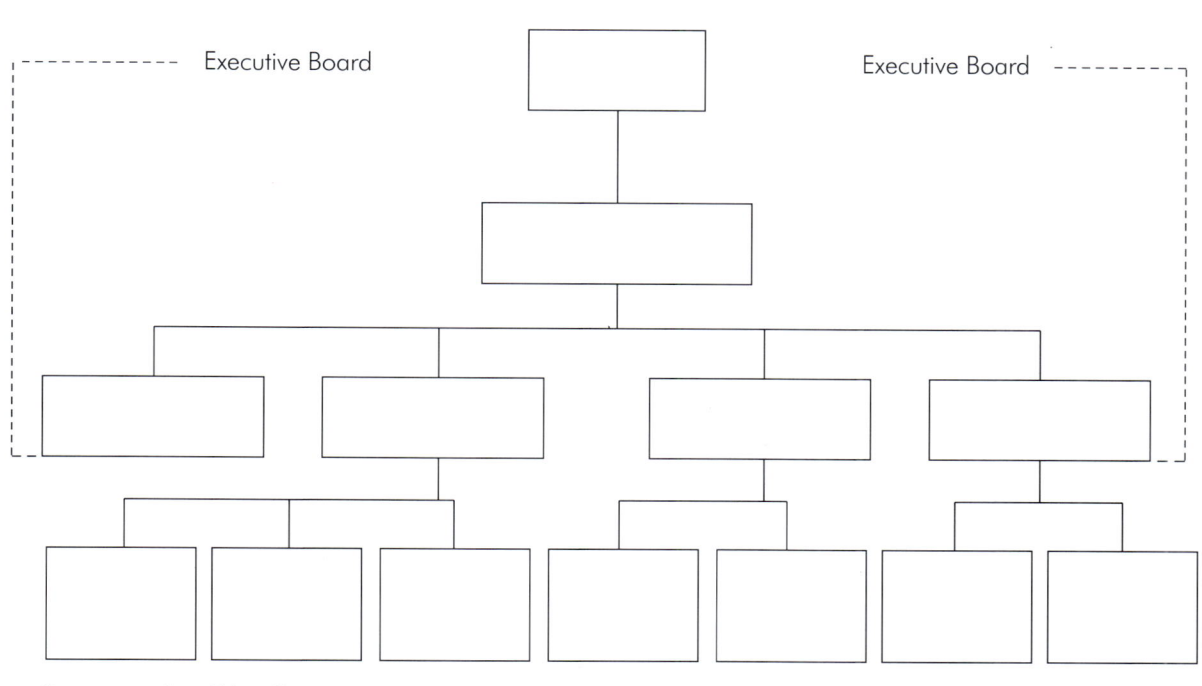

Organisation chart: Felton Computers

WORD CHECK

organisational structure	showing the way a company is organised
structure	organisation
Managing Director	director who is in charge of a whole company
executives	people who put decisions into action
personnel	staff
training	teaching employees how to do something
rationalisation	making more efficient
region	part of a country/an area
to split	to divide
matrix (basis)	organised according to two sets of criteria, e.g. geographical and functional
section	part of a company
subsidiary	company which is owned by a parent company
affiliate	company wholly or partly owned by another company

Unit 6

Supply

Describing product features

1. LISTENING Listen to the phone call about the supply of some office shelving systems. As you listen, fill in the missing information on the specification sheet.

Dimensions
Width ....
Height ....
Depth ....
Delivery
Cost ....
Time ....
Price
Unit price ....
Discount price for 10 units ....
Guarantee Period ....
Average life ....

2. PRESENTATION

In the telephone conversation the speakers discussed:

- dimensions
- time
- cost

Here is some of the language you heard.

2.1 Dimensions

Questions: How *wide* are they? (note the adjective form)
What's the *width*? (note the noun form)
How *high* are they?
What's the *height*?

Answers: They're 3.5 metres *wide*. (note the position of the adjective)
The *width* is 3.5 metres.
They're 2 metres *high*.
The *height* is 2 metres.

2.2 Time

Question: How long does it *take* after ordering? (note the verb)
Answer: It *takes* two weeks.

2.3 Cost

Questions: How much *is it*?
How much *does it cost*?
How much *do you charge*?

Answers: It's £98.
It *costs* £98.
We *charge* £98.

3. CONTROLLED PRACTICE

A. Complete the following table. Use a dictionary if necessary. The first one has been done for you.

Noun form	Adjective	Opposite adjective
width	*wide*	*narrow*
	long	
depth		
		low
distance		
speed		
reliability		

B. Ask questions about the technical and commercial specifications of the printer above. In all cases, use an *adjective* form with *How*.

1. The width of the printer   *How wide is it?*
2. The depth of the printer ....?
3. The speed of the printer ....?
4. The time to deliver ....?
5. The cost of delivery ....?
6. The reliability of the printer ....?
7. The length of the cable ....?
8. The length of the guarantee period ....?
9. The cost of the printer ....?
10. The distance to the nearest service centre ....?

4. TRANSFER

Pair work

Student B: Turn to the Key section.
Student A: Ask Student B for information about this personal computer and fill in the information on the specification sheet.

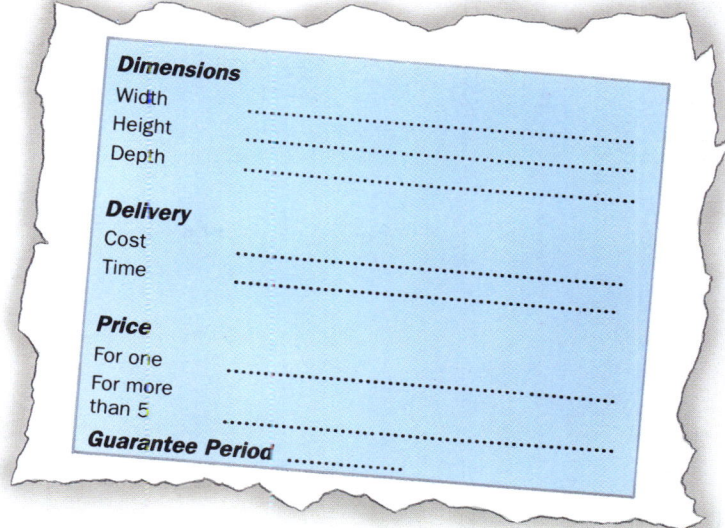

Dimensions
Width ....
Height ....
Depth ....

Delivery
Cost ....
Time ....

Price
For one ....
For more than 5 ....

Guarantee Period ....

WORD CHECK

shelving	rows of shelves
to enquire	to ask
specifications	detailed information
flexible	movable
to fit	to fix, to attach
to stick out	to reach a position further than is wanted
delivery	transportation of goods to a customer's address
to deliver	to transport goods to a customer's address
warehouse	large building where goods are stored
area	part of a town
charge	money which must be paid
to place an order	to order
guarantee	promise that something will work well
standard	normal
discount	percentage by which a seller reduces the full price for a buyer
to round ... off	to increase/decrease to the nearest full figure
sturdy	strong
average	normal

Unit 7

Making arrangements

Telephoning

1. LISTENING

Listen to the three telephone calls. As you listen, complete the table below.

Call	Name of person called	Name of caller	Reason for call	Result of call
1				
2				
3				

2. PRESENTATION

The telephone conversations you heard in the dialogues included a number of steps, in particular:

- identifying yourself/your company
- asking the caller to identify himself/herself
- asking for a connection
- taking/leaving a message
- explaining the reason for the call
- making appointments
- signing off

Now look at the language used in these steps.

2.1 Identifying yourself/your company
Krondike Electronics. Can I help you? (*a typical switchboard response*)
John Bird speaking.
This is Pete Edwards.
John here.

2.2 Asking the caller to identify himself/herself
Who's calling please?

2.3 Asking for a connection
I'd like to speak to _____, please.
Could you put me through to _____, please?
I'd like to speak to someone about deliveries, please.

— 35 —

2.4 Taking/leaving a message
I'm afraid he's out at the moment. Can I take a message?
Can you ask him to call me back?

2.5 Explaining the reason for the call
The reason I called is ……………………………….
I am (just) phoning to ……………………………….

2.6 Making appointments
Could you manage Tuesday?
What about Friday?
Shall we say two o'clock?
Just a moment, I'll get my diary.
I'm sorry, I'm out all day.
Friday would be fine.
That suits me.

2.7 Signing off
I look forward to seeing you.
Thanks for calling.
Goodbye.
Bye.

3. CONTROLLED PRACTICE

A. Put the following extracts of telephone calls into the correct order.

1.
- [ ] Just a moment, Mr Jones, I'll put you through.
- [ ] Yes, I'd like to speak to Miss Rathbone.
- [ ] Peter Jones.
- [ ] Who's calling, please?
- [ ] Pan Electronics. Can I help you?

2.
- [ ] She's got it, but just in case, it's 071-253 4686.
- [ ] Yes, could you ask her to call me back?
- [ ] Mr Gottman here. Could I speak to Mrs Fields?
- [ ] Yes, of course. Could I have your number?
- [ ] I'm afraid she's out at the moment. Can I take a message?

3.
- [ ] I'm sorry, I'm out on Wednesday.
- [ ] Good, that suits me too. Shall we say 11 o'clock?
- [ ] Just a moment, I'll get my diary … you said next week?
- [ ] Yes, could you manage Wednesday?
- [ ] What about Thursday then?
- [ ] Yes, Thursday morning would suit me fine.

4. Transfer

Pair work
Student B: Turn to the Key section.
Student A:

1. You are A Peterson. Telephone Student B and ask to speak to B Rogers (you can use the title Mr/Mrs/Miss/Ms or their first name). You want to speak to him/her about an order. Your telephone number is (0732) 435501.

2. B Rogers calls you back. You want to order some shoes. Before you order you would like to know the price for 10 pairs of model A293. Confirm the price and tell him/her you will fax the order right away.

3. You are A Taylor. Telephone Student B (B Dunn) to arrange a meeting to discuss your visit to Japan. You want to meet next week. Below is your diary for next week.

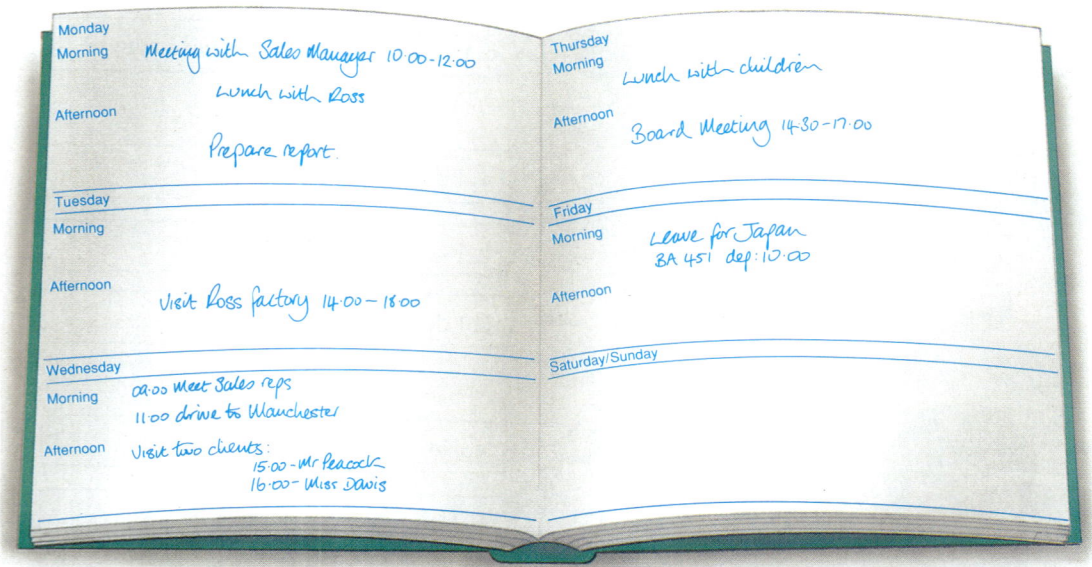

WORD CHECK

installation	the process of putting new machines into an office or a factory
complicated	difficult
technician	skilled technical worker
to sort out	to put right
to fix	to arrange
to manage	to be able to do something, e.g. meet on Tuesday
to suit	to be suitable or convenient

Unit 8

Information handling

Checking and confirming

1. LISTENING

When telephoning, it is very important to get certain facts right, for example, the name, address, and telephone number. Listen to the following telephone call twice. The first time, listen to it from the point of view of the caller and complete his notes below. The second time, listen to it from the point of view of the person who answered and complete his notes.

First listening: Caller's notes

Name of Company: Priority Investments
Name of Corporate Finance Manager:
Date of appointment:
Time of appointment:

Second listening: Called person's notes

RECORD OF PHONE CALL
Caller's name:
Caller's company:
Caller's address:

Telephone number:
Reason for call:
Date of appointment:
Time of appointment:
Action: 1. Confirm appointment with Mr Foster
2. Send

2. Presentation

In the telephone conversation the speakers followed a number of steps when handling and exchanging information, in particular:

- clarifying information
- asking for repetition
- asking for spelling
- showing understanding
- correcting information
- confirming information
- acknowledging

Now look at the language used to handle information.

2.1 Clarifying information
Could you tell me exactly what … ?

2.2 Asking for repetition
Could I have your name again, please?
Could you repeat that?
I'm sorry, I didn't catch that.

2.3 Asking for spelling
Could you spell that, please?

2.4 Showing understanding
I see.
I've got that.
Right.

2.5 Correcting information
No, not Seanew. Sea*view*.
That's not right, it's … .

2.6 Confirming information
Let me just repeat that, … .

2.7 Acknowledging
That's right.

Notes: 1. Saying and repeating telephone numbers:

Look at the number: 081-455 2354.

The number consists of three groups.
0 is pronounced 'oh' or zero;
455 is verbalised as four double five or four five five;
the numbers should be grouped, e.g. 081 pause 455 pause 2354.

2. Spelling names:

A useful way to remember the pronunciation of some letters is to group them by vowel sound:

ay	ee	e	y	oh	u	ar
A	B	F	I	O	Q	R
H	C	L	Y		U	
J	D	M			W	
K	E	N				
	G	S				
	P	X				
	T	(UK) Z (zed)				
	V					
	(US) Z					

3. CONTROLLED PRACTICE

A. Complete these dialogues.

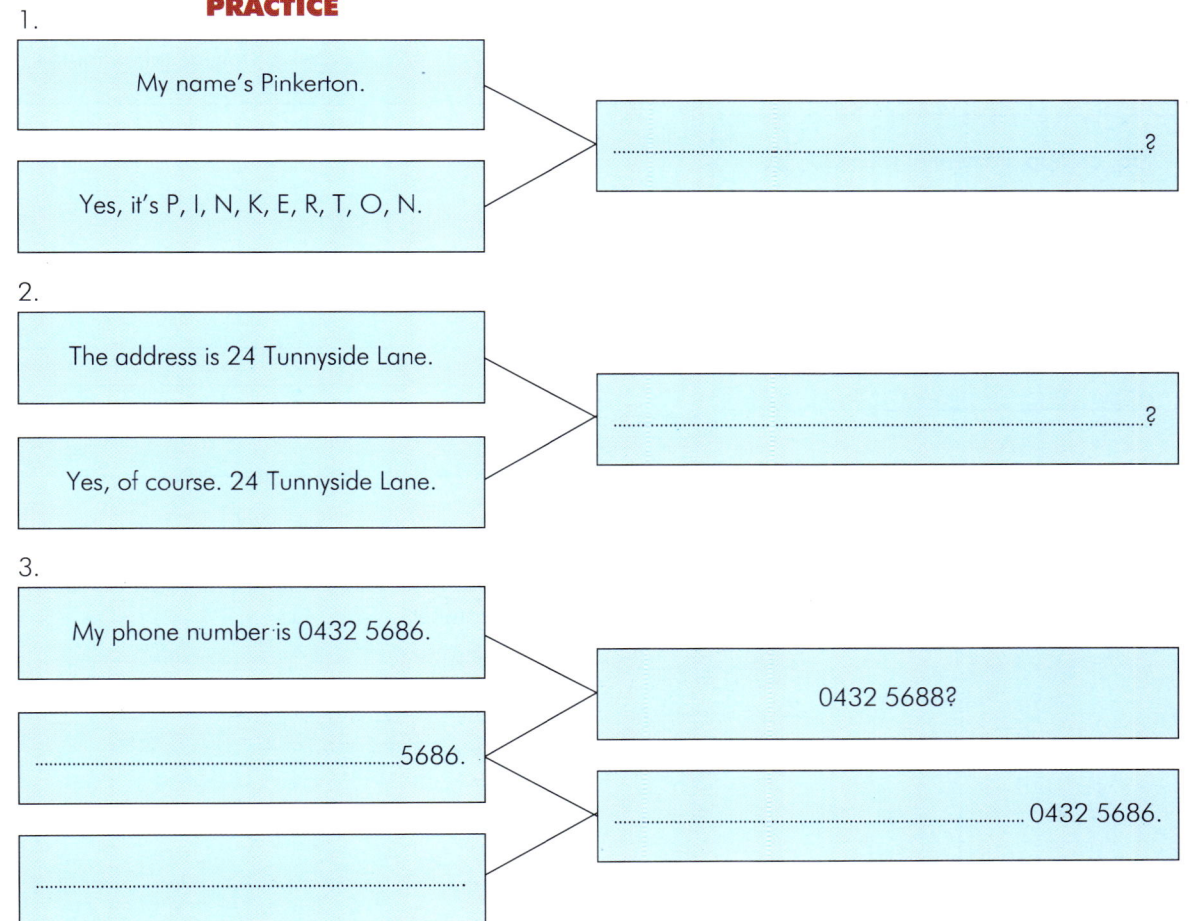

1.
- My name's Pinkerton.
- ....?
- Yes, it's P, I, N, K, E, R, T, O, N.

2.
- The address is 24 Tunnyside Lane.
- ....?
- Yes, of course. 24 Tunnyside Lane.

3.
- My phone number is 0432 5686.
- 0432 5688?
- .... 5686.
- .... 0432 5686.
- ....

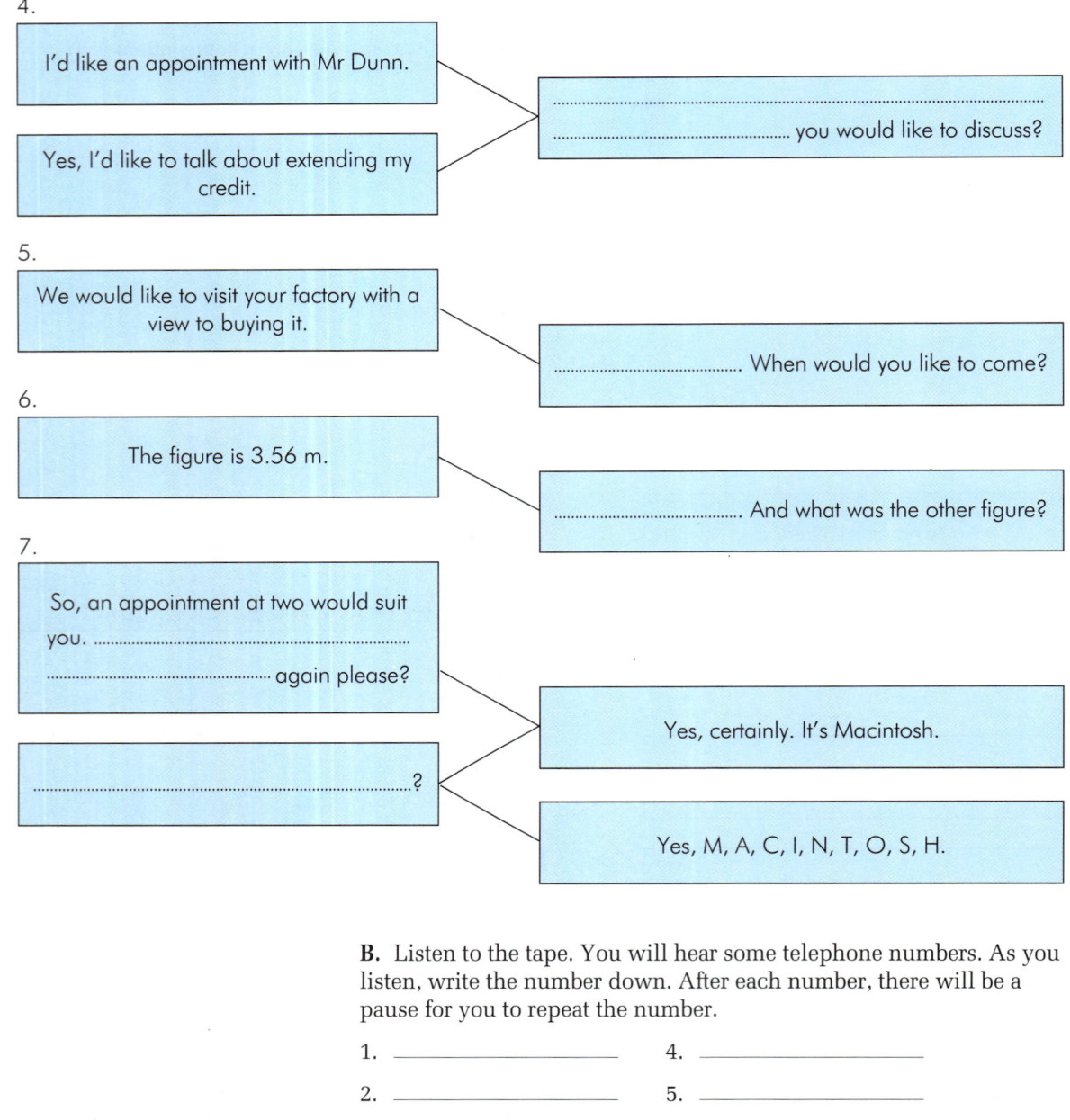

B. Listen to the tape. You will hear some telephone numbers. As you listen, write the number down. After each number, there will be a pause for you to repeat the number.

1. _____   4. _____

2. _____   5. _____

3. _____   6. _____

C. Listen to the tape. You will hear some names and then a request to spell them. There is a pause on the tape for you to spell them and then you will hear the correct spelling. The names are:

1. Peterson
2. Hardy
3. Glynis
4. Matthews
5. Rifkind
6. Thatcher
7. Samuel
8. Marjorie

Now listen to the tape again. This time, cover up the names above and write them down when you hear them spelt.

1. _____
2. _____
3. _____
4. _____
5. _____
6. _____
7. _____
8. _____

4. Transfer

Pair work
Student B: Turn to the Key section.
Student A:
1. You are D Roth (you can use the title Mr/Mrs/Miss/Ms or a first name). You work for Sellersdown Sports Shop. Their address is 23 North Riding Road, Brentwood, CM14 5TU. Their phone number is 0277 239 456.

Phone Newsome Sports Ltd. Ask the price of the following items and then place an order. Tell them you want the order to be delivered on or before 10 September.

50 pairs of training shoes
30 pairs of socks
10 Greys squash rackets

Cost: 1 pair of training shoes _____

   1 pair of socks _____

   1 Greys racket _____

Order number _____

2. You work for SkiWear Plus. Student B is going to phone you and place an order. Fill in the invoice overleaf. Some of it has been done for you. When you have taken the order, give your customer the order number.

SkiWear Plus
22 Richmond Rd.
York YO1 1PN

VAT Registration number: 223 7634 29

Order No. 463 XL

Description	Unit price	Quantity	Price
White ski hat	£5.00		
Green ski hat	£4.50		112.50
Leather ski gloves	£12.00		
		Total price	602.50

Delivery date ....
Payment terms ....
Delivery address ....
....
....

Contact name ....
phone ....

WORD CHECK

corporate	referring to a whole company
appointment	arrangement to meet
to approach	to contact someone
investment	placing of money so that it will increase in value
convenient	suitable
to suit	to be suitable or convenient
current	present
prospectus	document which gives information to buyers or customers

Unit 9

Job routines

Present simple and expressions of frequency

1. LISTENING You will hear an interview between a journalist and a top businessman. The journalist is going to write an article called 'A day in the life of Paul Johnson'.

First look at the different activities below. Then, as you listen, number the sequence of events in Paul Johnson's typical day. Some of them have been done for you.

a. ☐ Visit the plant
b. ☐ Look at the post
c. ☐ Have breakfast
d. ☐ Meetings with Finance and Sales Directors
e. ☐ Read a book
f. [1] Get up
g. ☐ Dinner engagement
h. ☐ Leave for the office
i. ☐ Go for a jog
j. ☐ Lunch in the canteen
k. [11] Management/ Board meetings
l. [4] Read the newspapers
m. ☐ Meeting with deputy
n. ☐ Finish work
o. ☐ Go to sleep

2. PRESENTATION

There are two important features of the language used in the interview:

- the present simple tense
- expressions of frequency

2.1 The present simple tense

This is used when we talk about *characteristic/typical* actions.
e.g. He *gets up* at 5.
I *read* the newspapers after breakfast.

Note: The third person singular form ends in *s*.

We form questions in the present simple by using the auxiliary *do*.
e.g. When *do* you go to bed?
Does your wife work too?

Note: The third person singular form is *does*.

2.2 Expressions of frequency

Expressions of frequency are divided into indefinite and definite frequency.

Indefinite frequency

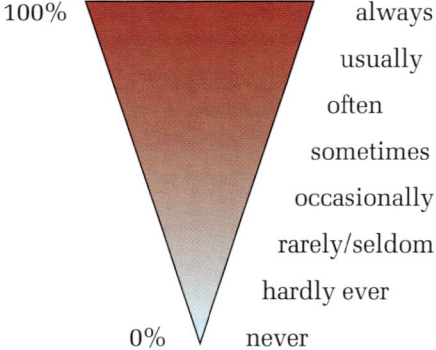

100% always
usually
often
sometimes
occasionally
rarely/seldom
hardly ever
0% never

Notes:
1. The percentage triangle shows the relative frequency of these expressions. Of course, these percentages are only a general indication, not exact values.
2. Expressions of indefinite frequency are usually used with the present simple.
   e.g. I often go down to our plant.
3. Notice the position of the adverbs of indefinite frequency with the verb *to be* and other verbs.
   e.g. I'm *usually* behind my desk by 7.30. (adverb after verb 'to be')
   We *usually* have breakfast around 6.30. (adverb before the verb)
   Sometimes I have lunch out with customers. (adverb at the beginning of the sentence)

Definite frequency

every day	or	daily
every week		weekly
every month		monthly
every year		yearly/annually

once/twice/three times a day/week/month/year etc.

3. CONTROLLED PRACTICE

A. Complete the dialogue with an appropriate question. The first one has been done for you.

A: *When do you get up?*
B: Usually at six. At least, my alarm clock goes off at six!
A: ....?
B: No, I don't have breakfast straight away; first I go for a run.
A: ....?
B: I sit down for breakfast about seven.
A: ....?
B: After breakfast I read the papers.
A: ....?
B: Oh, *The Guardian* and *The Independent*.
A: ....?
B: I usually leave for the office about eight and I'm behind my desk by eight-thirty.
A: ....?
B: I sort through the mail first.
A: ....?
B: No, I don't have a secretary. I wish I had!
A: ....?
B: No, I sometimes travel abroad.
A: ....?
B: Oh, about four times a year. Usually to America.

— 47 —

B. Change the following sentences using an expression of indefinite frequency as indicated by the number in brackets.

e.g. I sort through my mail. (100%)
       I *always* sort through my mail.

1. I travel abroad. (40%)
   ....

2. I have meetings. (75%).
   ....

3. I see the Managing Director. (50%)
   ....

4. I see the Chairman. (10%)
   ....

5. I catch the seven o'clock bus. (100%)
   ....

4. Transfer

Pair work

Interview your partner. Find out about his/her daily routines.

WORD CHECK

interview	meeting to ask a person questions in order to collect information
journalist	person who writes for a newspaper
event	happening
jog	run
cover	front and back pages of a newspaper or book
post	mail, letters
to sort out	to put in order
attention	action
deputy	person who takes the place of another
agenda	list of things to be done
up-to-date	informed of the latest information
canteen	factory restaurant
plant	factory
committee	official group of people who plan or organise for a larger group
board meeting	meeting of the directors of a company
engagement	appointment to do something, e.g. go out for dinner
midnight	12 o'clock at night

Unit 10

Current projects

Present continuous

1. LISTENING

The Managing Director is getting up-to-date on the current projects of various departments. In some cases, they have no current projects, but have fixed plans for the future. As you listen, match the projects/plans with the departments. The first one has been done for you.

PROJECTS/FIXED PLANS
- plan advertising campaign
- test new prototype
- move to new offices
- do user study
- rationalise distribution network
- run quality training seminars
- look into new accounting system
- try to recruit new graduates
- install automated assembly line

DEPARTMENTS
EDP
Finance
Marketing
Production
Personnel
Administration
Research and Development
Transport
Management Services

2. PRESENTATION

In this extract, you heard the present continuous tense used in two ways:

> to indicate the present (and temporary) nature of the activity

> to indicate that a future plan is fixed (cannot be changed)

2.1 To indicate the present (and temporary) nature of the activity
We *are doing* a user study at the moment.
We *are* currently *installing* the new assembly line.

Note: Time markers like: *at the moment, currently, now* are often used.

— 50 —

2.2 To indicate that a future plan is fixed (cannot be changed)
We *are moving* to new offices next week.
We *are running* a series of quality training seminars next month.

Note: We use the present continuous to mean a present fixed plan to do something in the future.

3. CONTROLLED PRACTICE

A. Complete the tapescript of a meeting by inserting the right form. Use each of the following verbs once:

| work on | find | run at | come | do | happen | plan |
| approach | reach | think | expand | manage |

MD: At the moment, the market _____ _____. So this is an opportunity we must take. Our advertising agency _____ _____ _____ a new campaign for next month. Now, what about Production?

PM: Currently we _____ _____ _____ 75% capacity — so, that gives us some spare capacity.

MD: Good, how _____ we _____ on staffing levels in the factory?

PM: We _____ it difficult to recruit technicians. There seems to be a shortage on the job market.

MD: What _____ you _____ to do about it?

PM: Well, we _____ of using a recruitment agency. A chap from a local agency _____ in to see me on Monday to talk about it.

MD: Fine, what about cash flow? The upturn in the market is going to be a drain on cash.

FM: That's right. At the moment, we _____ on an overdraft of about £50,000 and our current debts _____ £85,000. I can go and talk to the Bank Manager about it. We've always been a good customer.

MD: Yes, do that as soon as possible. Finally, training. We're going to need some more sales reps and technicians in production. What _____ at the moment in training?

TM: We _____ a refresher sales course but we've got spare capacity …

B. Sylvia Drake and Michael Moore are arranging a meeting to discuss next year's sales budget. Look at their diaries for Monday to Wednesday and complete the conversation. Use the verbs in the box in the present continuous form.

> pick up   have   show   give   go   discuss   work

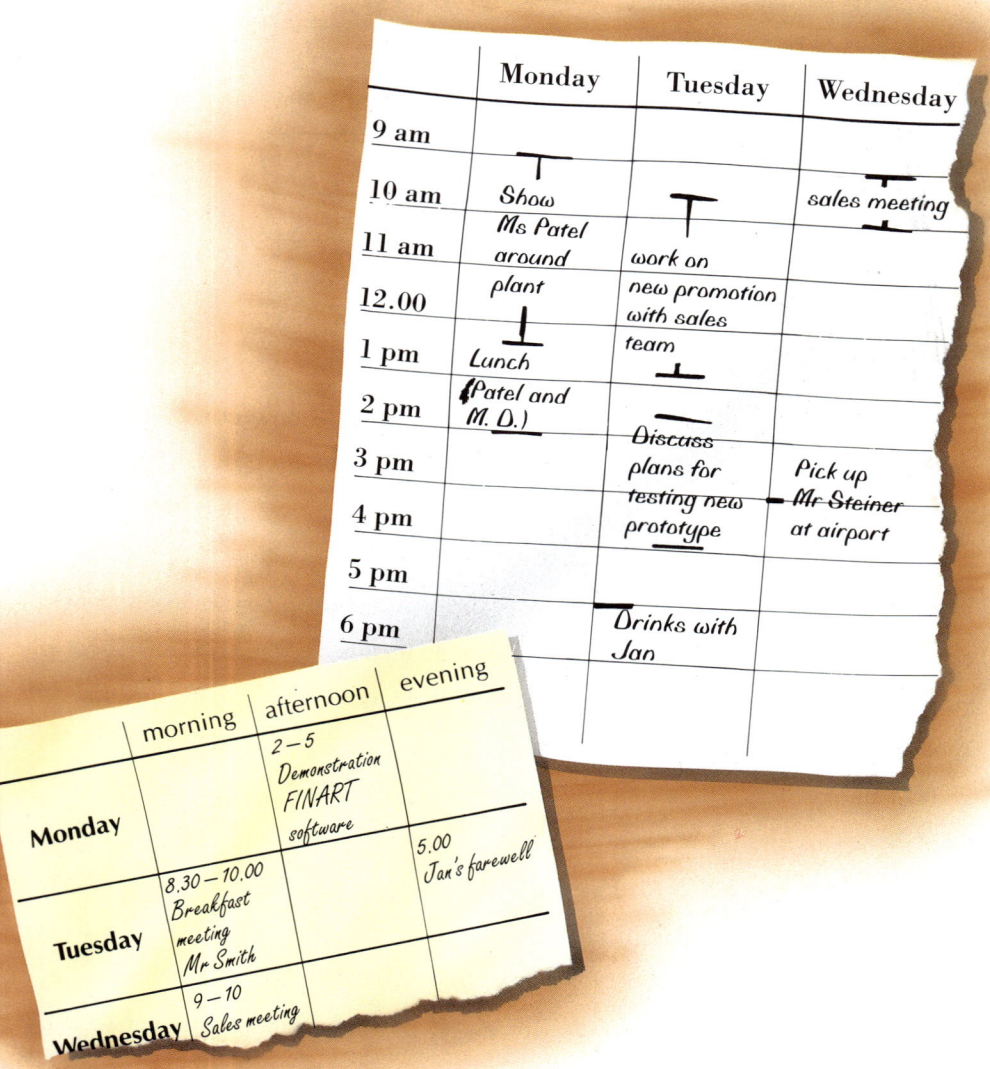

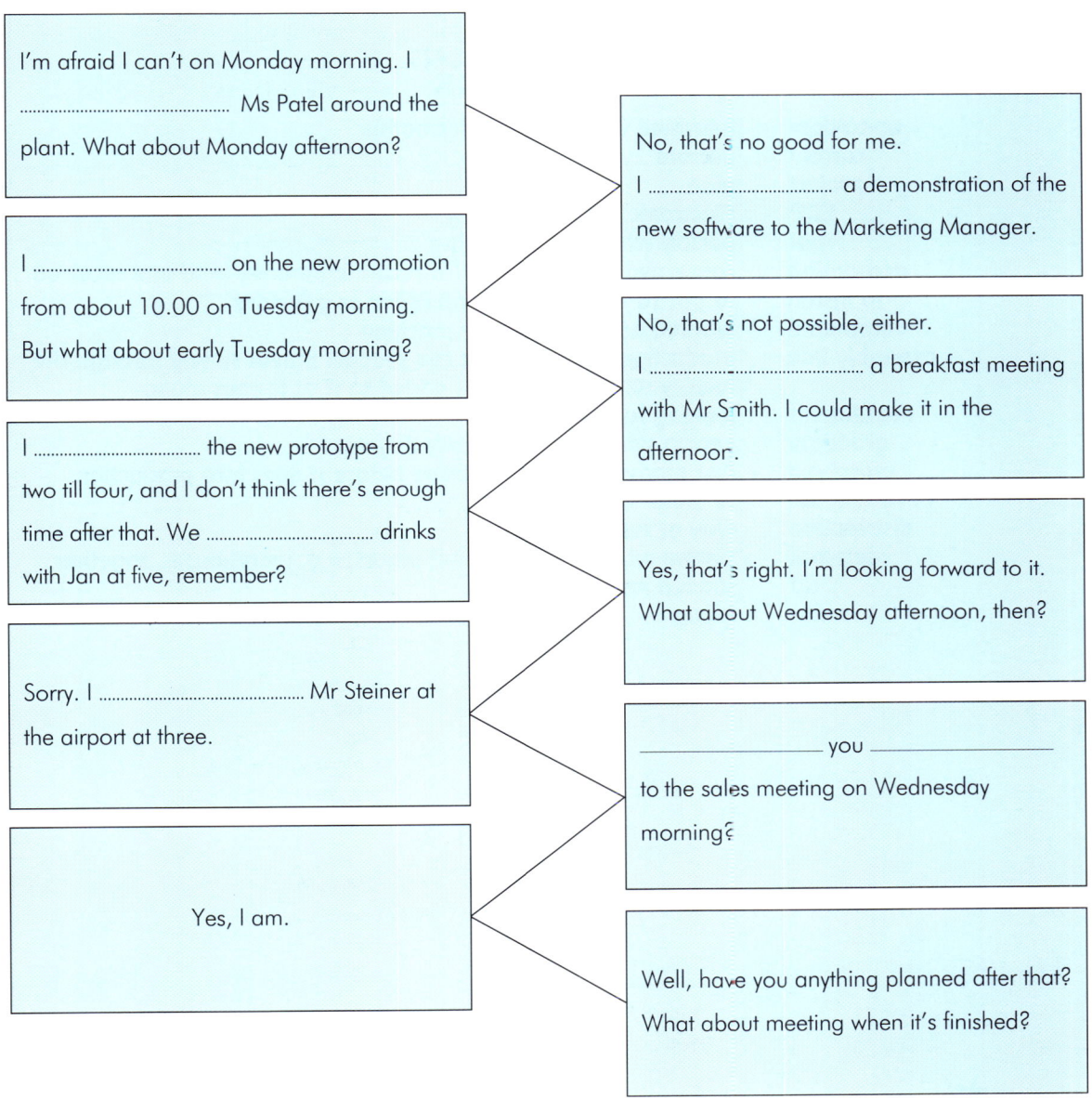

4. TRANSFER

Group work

Ask the other members of the group:

1. What current work they are involved in.
2. What fixed plans they have for the future.

WORD CHECK

up-to-date	informed of the latest information
current	present
project	plan
EDP	Electronic Data Processing
user	person who uses something
accounting	concerned with the work of recording money paid and received
to install	to put (a machine) into an office or a factory
automated	worked automatically by machine
assembly line	production system where the product moves slowly through the factory with new sections added to it as it goes along
recruitment	looking for new staff
graduate	person who has a university degree
prototype	first model of a new machine before it goes into production
to rationalise	to make more efficient
distribution	way of sending goods
network	system which links different places, e.g. warehouses, together
cut	sudden lowering of costs
series	group

Unit 11

Business correspondence

Letter writing

1. LISTENING First read the letters below. Then listen to the three telephone calls. As you listen, match the telephone calls with the letters.

Letter A: Telephone call _____

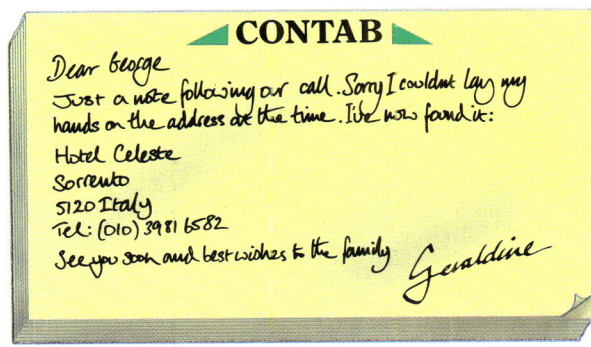

Letter B: Telephone call _____

Letter C: Telephone call

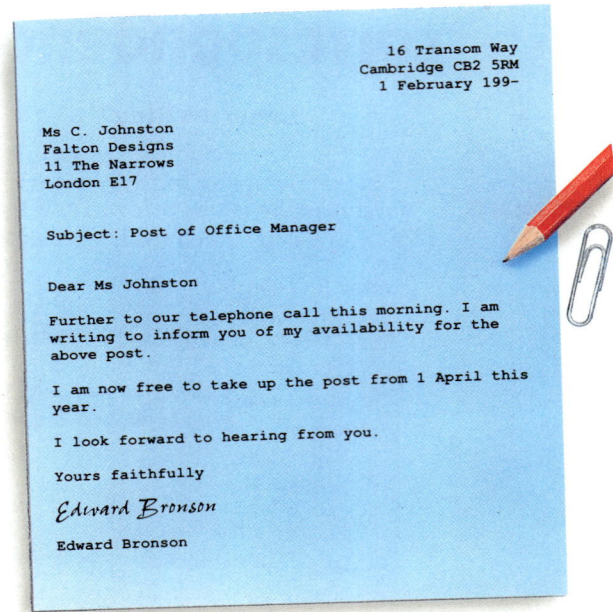

2. Presentation

Business letters typically contain the following features (although they may not all appear in the same letter):

- opening and closing greetings
- stating the reference at the beginning of the letter
- requesting
- explaining the reason for writing
- thanking
- enclosing documents
- apologising
- expressing urgency
- confirming
- ending the letter

Here is some of the language typical of business letters.

2.1 Opening and closing greetings

If you don't have a contact name:

Dear Sir or Madam
Yours faithfully

If you know the name of the person:

Dr Mr Jones
    Mrs
    Miss
    Ms
Yours sincerely

If you know the person as a friend or close business colleague:

Dear James
Best wishes/Regards

2.2   Stating the reference at the beginning of the letter
You can start with either:

Subject: ………………………………………

Reference: ………………………………………

Re: ………………………………

or an expression like:

With reference to …
I thank you for your letter of 1 July.
Further to our telephone conversation, …

2.3   Requesting
I would be grateful if you could …
I would appreciate it if you could …
Could you please … ? (more informal)

2.4   Explaining the reason for writing
I am writing to inform you that/apply for/request, etc. …

2.5   Thanking
Thank you for …
We were very pleased to …

2.6   Enclosing documents
Where other documents are included with the letter, you can say:

Please find enclosed/attached …

2.7   Apologising
I regret that …
I am afraid that …
I am sorry that …
I apologise for …

2.8   Expressing urgency
… at your earliest convenience
… without delay
… as soon as possible

2.9 Confirming
I am pleased to confirm that …
I confirm that …
This is to confirm that …

2.10 Ending the letter
I look forward to …
I am sure that …
I hope …
See you soon. (informal)

3. CONTROLLED PRACTICE

A. Select expressions from the Presentation section according to the prompts given in brackets to complete the letter.

Rainbow Training Institute
53 Bradburn Close
Muswell Hill
London N10 1PJ

Phone 081 883 2555
Fax 081 884 9345

J Fisher
The Personnel Manager
DJ Banking Corp.
54 Smithson Ave
London E17 6TY

20 September 199–

Re: International Sales Workshop 5 November

Dear Ms Fisher

_____ (*explaining the reason for writing*), unfortunately we have had to cancel our November workshop. However, we can include your staff in the October 8 workshop instead if this is convenient.

_____ (*apologising*) we were unable to inform you of this change earlier, and I hope you will be able to attend at this earlier date.

_____ (*requesting*) let me know _____ (*expressing urgency*) the names of your staff who will be attending on October 8.

_____ (*ending*) your staff will find the workshop both useful and informative.

Yours _____ (*closing*)

T Reading

T Reading
Training Manager

B. Complete the fax which was sent in reply to the letter in A.

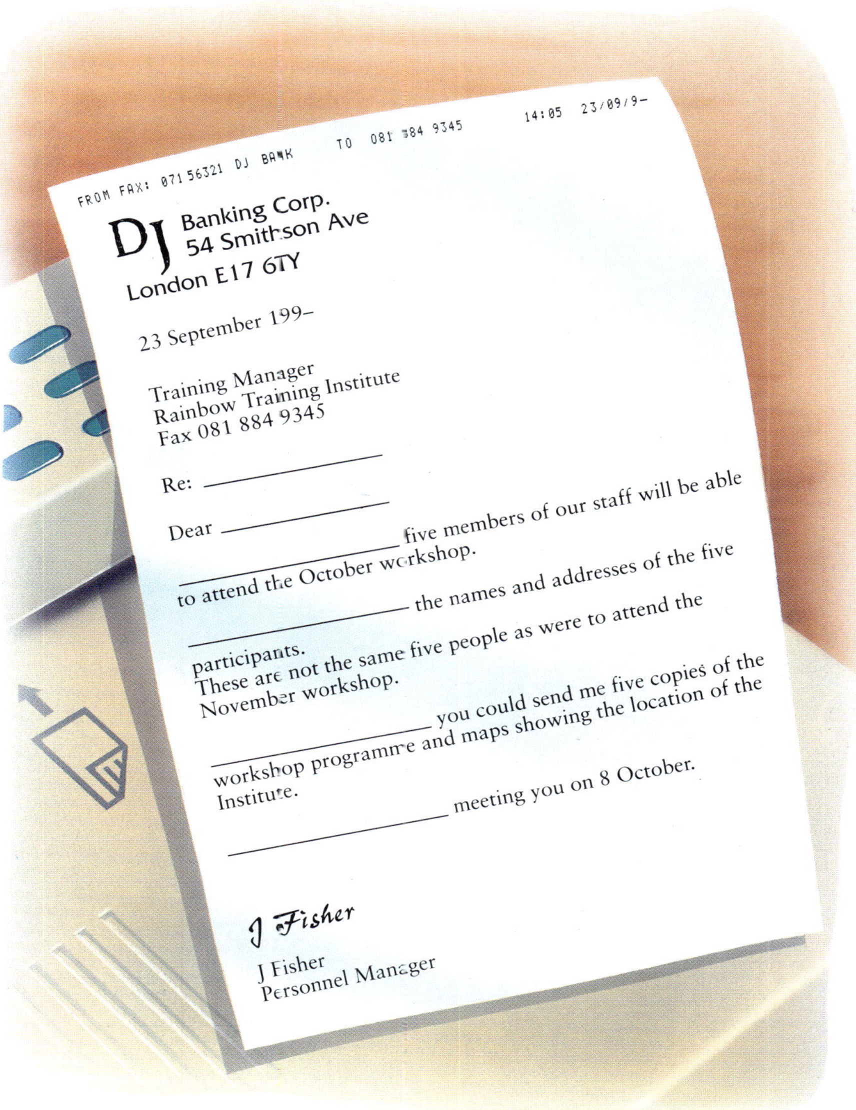

FROM FAX: 071 56321 DJ BANK   TO 081 884 9345   14:05 23/09/9–

DJ Banking Corp.
54 Smithson Ave
London E17 6TY

23 September 199–

Training Manager
Rainbow Training Institute
Fax 081 884 9345

Re: _____

Dear _____ five members of our staff will be able to attend the October workshop.

_____ the names and addresses of the five participants.

These are not the same five people as were to attend the November workshop.

_____ you could send me five copies of the workshop programme and maps showing the location of the Institute.

_____ meeting you on 8 October.

J Fisher

J Fisher
Personnel Manager

4. TRANSFER   Write a reply to the following letter.

Your reply should include the following:

- reference to the above letter
- confirmation of your participation
- request for more information about the programme
- apology for not being able to give another presentation (pressure of work – no time for preparation)
- a polite phrase to end the letter.

Some parts of the letter have already been done for you.

WORD CHECK

LETTERS

to lay one's hands on	to find (informal)
consultancy	act of giving specialist advice
contract	legal agreement between two people or groups
quotation	estimate of how much something will cost
above-mentioned	something already referred to in a letter
to attach	to fasten, to link
due	expected, supposed
to appreciate	to be thankful or grateful
post	job
availability	state of being able to take up a new job

PHONE CALLS

to reply	to answer
urgently	immediately
to get back to	to phone again
to advertise	to announce publicly that a job is vacant
application	asking for something, e.g. a job, usually in writing
to recommend	to suggest
to drop a line	to write a short letter

Unit 12

Sales review

Describing graphs

1. LISTENING

Listen to the sales review. As you listen, match the model number of the product to the graph.

Models: A1456, B2456, C3456

Graph 1
Sales performance: Model _____

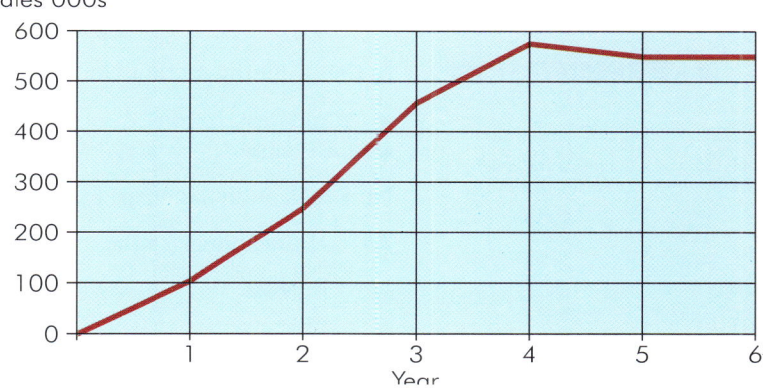

Graph 2
Sales performance: Model _____

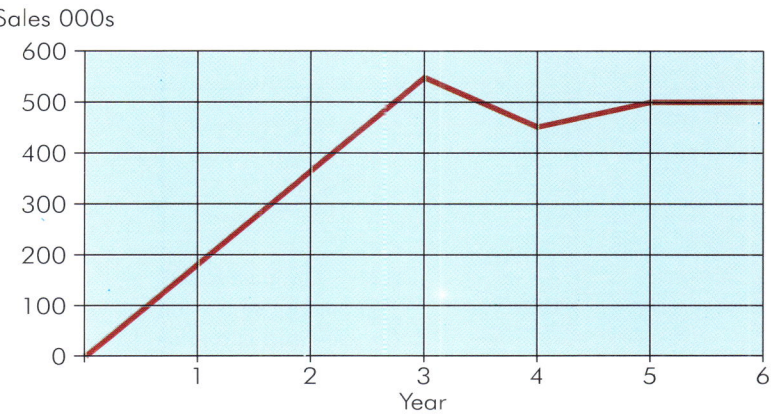

Graph 3
Sales performance: Model _____

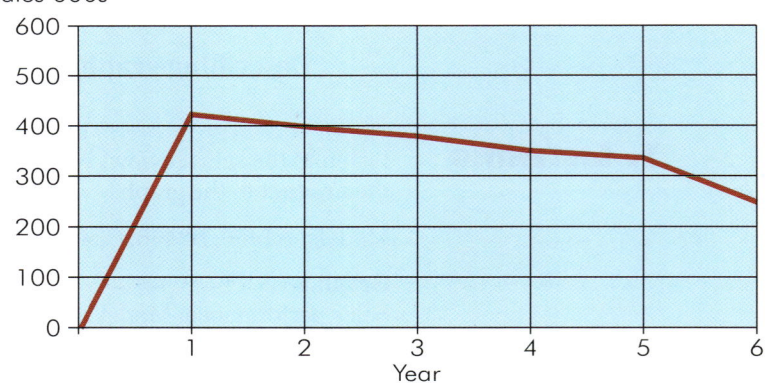

2. PRESENTATION

In the Listening section you heard a presentation which included:

- graph description
- past tenses

Now look at the language that the presenter used.

2.1 Describing graphs

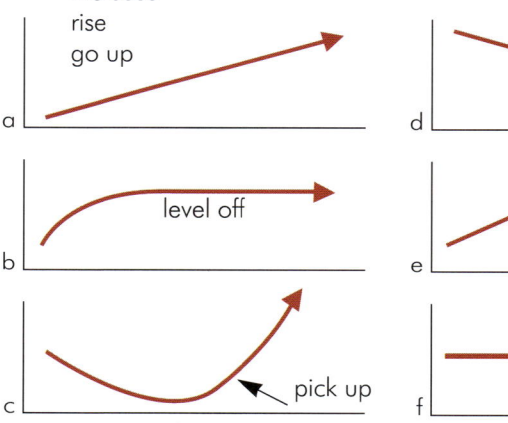

2.2 The past tense

The past tense is used throughout the extract because the time is *finished* and is marked by expressions like:

- 10 years ago
- in 1992
- by the end of 1991
- last year

Regular verbs end in *ed*	reach	→ reached
	remain	→ remained
	increase	→ increased
	drop	→ dropped
	level	→ levelled
Irregular verbs:	rise	→ rose
	fall	→ fell
	go	→ went
	be	→ was/were

3. CONTROLLED PRACTICE

Use the three graphs in the Listening section and the language in the Presentation section to complete the sentences.

A1456

1. Sales _____ a peak just one year after launch.
2. The following two years sales _____ _____ at 400,000.
3. Then sales _____ to a figure of 330,000 by the end of year five.
4. Last year sales _____ to only 250,000 units.

B2456

5. In the first three years, sales _____ steadily.
6. The following year sales _____ badly.
7. Then in year five they _____ _____ again.
8. They _____ at this figure in year six.

C3456

9. Sales _____ rapidly in the second year to reach 250,000.
10. In year three they _____ to 450,000.
11. Year four figures _____ _____ to 580,000.
12. In year five sales _____ slightly.

4. TRANSFER

Pair work
Student B: Turn to the Key section.
Student A:
1. The graph on the following page shows the performance of a product (sales and prices) over the last six years. Describe it to Student B.

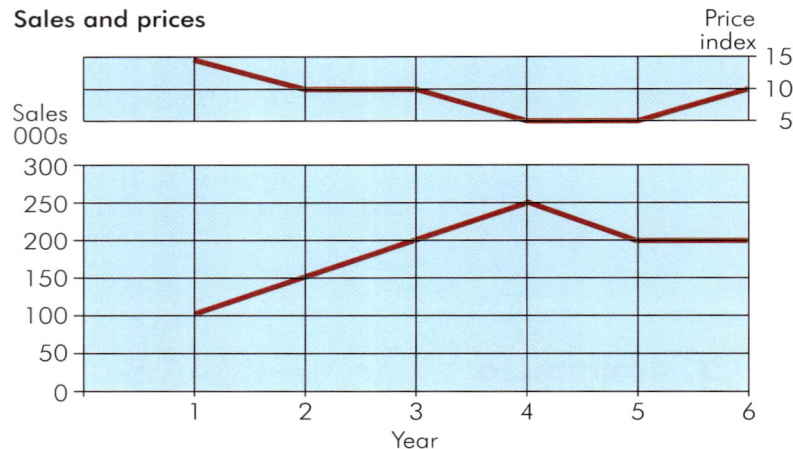

2. Now listen to Student B's description of the performance of a product. As you listen complete the graph below.

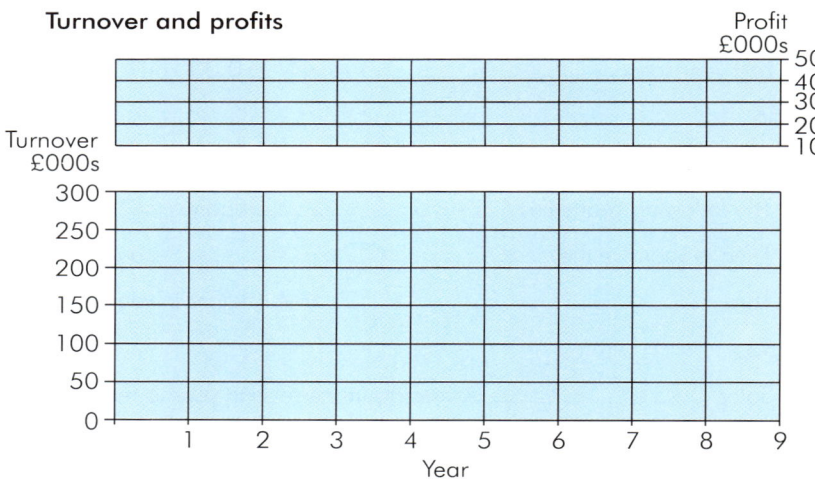

WORD CHECK

target	level, e.g. of sales, to aim for
performance	how good or bad the results are
product	thing which is made or manufactured
to launch	to put a new product on the market
peak	highest point
unit	single product
steadily	in a regular or continuous way
to settle	to stay at the same level
rapidly	quickly
slightly	not very much, a little
results	outcome of the year's trading

Unit 13

Sales forecasts

Intentions and predictions

1. LISTENING   A Sales Director presents the sales targets for four products. As you listen, match the graphs with the model numbers of the products.
Models: A1456, B2456, C3456, D4456

Graph 1
Sales target: Model _____

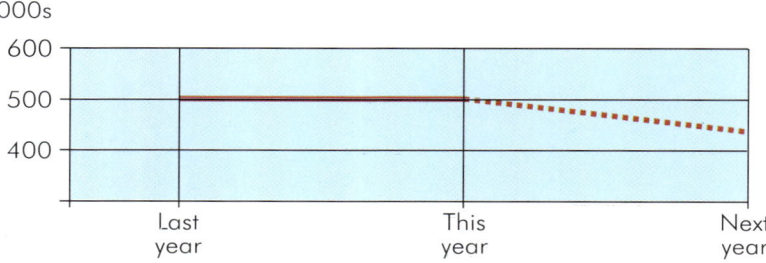

Graph 2
Sales target: Model _____

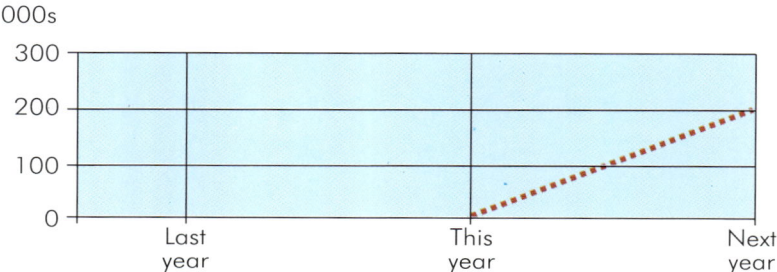

Graph 3
Sales target: Model

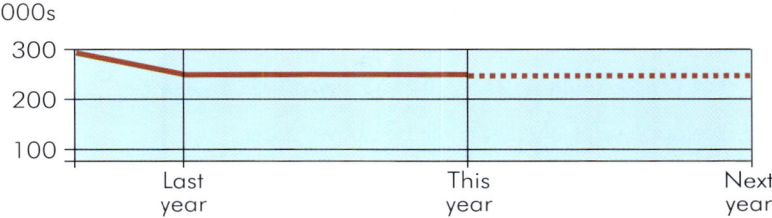

Graph 4
Sales target: Model _____

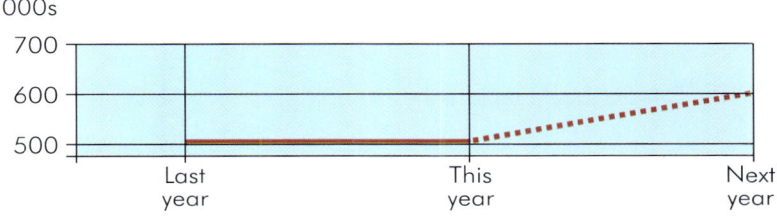

2. PRESENTATION

When we talk about the future, we can do so either personally or impersonally. We can also indicate the degree of probability in terms of:

- certainty
- probability
- possibility

Now look at the language used in the Listening section.

Personal form	Impersonal form	Likelihood
We are sure sales will rise We intend to increase sales	Sales will (certainly) rise Sales are going to rise	Certainty
We expect sales will rise We think sales will rise	Sales should rise Sales will probably rise	Probability
We hope sales will rise	Sales may rise Sales could rise	Possibility

3. CONTROLLED PRACTICE

Use the language in the Presentation section to change these sentences into the equivalent personal or impersonal form. The first one has been done for you.

1. Sales of B2456 will probably reach their target.

   We expect/think sales of B2456 will reach their target. (personal form)

2. We hope sales of A1456 will be above target.

   .... (impersonal form)

3. We intend to launch the D4456 next year.

   .... (impersonal form)

4. We are sure that C3456 sales will reach their target.

   .... (impersonal form)

5. The D4456 should replace the A1456.

   .... (personal form)

6. We hope the new medium-range product will be ready in two years' time.

   .... (impersonal form)

7. The sales team intend to carry out a large-scale promotion campaign.

   .... (impersonal form)

8. Total sales could be around £1,250,000 next year.

   .... (personal form)

9. We think the campaign will be successful.

   .... (impersonal form)

10. The R & D department hope to have the product ready in five years' time.

    .... (impersonal form)

4. TRANSFER

Pair work
Student B: Turn to the Key section.
Student A:
1. You are a customer. Phone your supplier (Student B) and find out about the delivery dates of the following products. Note down the degree of likelihood of the supplier keeping to these dates.

Product	Delivery date	Likelihood
office desks		
office chairs		
calendars		
year planners		
filing cabinets		
security cupboards		

Ask questions like: When can we expect delivery?
When do you think ... ?

When you have finished, compare your notes with Student B's information.

2. You are a supplier of computer products. A customer (Student B) will telephone you about delivery dates. Use the information below to answer his/her questions. Use the language from the Presentation section to indicate the degree of likelihood.

Product	Delivery date	Likelihood
adjustable keyboard	23 June	certainty
mouse	7 May	probability
colour scanner	20 July	possibility
colour printer	23 June	probability
floppy discs	1 May	certainty
21-inch colour screen	3 August	possibility

WORD CHECK

target	level to aim for
roughly	about, approximately
large-scale	working in a large way
promotion	advertising, publicity
to push	to promote vigorously
optimistic	feeling sure that things will work out well
to achieve	to succeed in doing something
medium-term	referring to a period of about five years
to launch	to put a new product on the market
to take off	to start to rise quickly, to be a success (new product)
medium-range	of middle price or size, suitable for the middle of the market

Unit 14

Company results

Present perfect v. past simple

1. LISTENING Listen to a company chairman making an end-of-year presentation. As you listen, complete his presentation notes.

End of year review
3 areas
1. Financial   a. Results   • turnover + 14%
                            • costs _____
                            • profits _____
              b. Exports – _____
                 Domestic market - very competitive, only _____
2. Personnel a. Personnel development continued
              b. 72 recruited
                 20 retired
                 52 net increase
              c. _____ has expanded
                 new areas: quality assurance and _____
3. Technology a. Research Dept has _____ prototype engine
              b. Have _____ technology programme

2. PRESENTATION

In his presentation, the chairman used the present perfect tense (*has/have* + past participle).
e.g. The results *have been* very pleasing.
      The company *has performed* well.

He uses this tense because:

1. He is probably talking at the end of December – the year is not quite finished.

2. He doesn't specifically refer to time periods. Contrast the present perfect and the past simple in the following sentences:
   The company *has performed* well. (present perfect)
   The company *performed* well at the beginning of the year. (past simple)

3. Many of the events have a present impact.
e.g. We *have invested* heavily in the European technology programme.

So, we can contrast the present perfect with the past simple, as follows:

Present perfect	Past simple
We have done well this year. *time unfinished*	We did well last year. *time finished*
I've been to Paris. *time not stated*	I went to Paris last week. *time stated*
Our research department has thoroughly tested the new prototype. *present and future impact*	Our research department thoroughly tested the new prototype and found it was not effective. *no present impact*

3. CONTROLLED PRACTICE

A. Put the verbs in brackets into an appropriate tense – present perfect or past simple.

1. Turnover .... by 14% last year. (*increase*)
2. The company .... disappointing results recently. (*have*)
3. The domestic consumer market .... very competitive. (*be*)
4. Two years ago we .... an updated product. (*launch*)
5. We .... 20 junior managers. (*recruit*)

6. .... you ever .... Australia? (*visit*)
7. We .... there last June. (*go*)
8. We .... not .... the results of the tests yet. (*receive*)
9. .... you .... the report? (*see*) Yes, it was interesting.
10. Three senior managers .... this year. (*retire*)

B. Complete the chart below.

Irregular verbs

Present simple/ infinitive	Past simple	Past participle
do	*did*	*done*
drive		
eat		
fly		
go		
have		
make		
send		
sleep		
speak		
write		

4. TRANSFER

Pair work
Student B: Turn to the Key section.
Student A:
1. Find out whether Student B has or hasn't done the things in the list below. If the answer is yes, ask for further information about when/where/why he/she did them.

All the introductory questions should be in the present perfect. All the questions for further information (when/where/why etc.) should be in the past simple.
    e.g. Have you (ever) travelled by hovercraft?
          Where did you go to?
          When was that?
          Why did you go there?

1. Work abroad
2. Visit America
3. Chair a meeting
4. Make a presentation in English
5. Speak on the telephone in English
6. Fly on Concorde
7. Sleep in a tent
8. Drive a car on the left-hand side of the road.

2. Student B is now going to ask you some questions. Your answers should be in either the present perfect or past simple.

WORD CHECK

chairman	person who is in charge of a meeting
review	general examination
results	outcome of the year's trading
turnover	amount of sales
to drop	to fall
profits	money gained which is more than money spent
domestic	home
competitive	difficult, as a result of the activities of other companies in the same area
disappointing	below expectation
policy	decisions on the way of doing something
actually	in fact
to recruit	to get new staff
to expand	to get bigger
quality assurance	checking that the quality of a product is good
growth	increase in size
prototype	first model of a new machine before it goes into production

Unit 15

Company strategy

Conditional 1

1. LISTENING

Listen to the discussion about company strategy. Match the conditions to the results. The first one has been done for you.

Conditions
1. Reduce prices
2. Margins smaller
3. Increase production
4. Invest in new plant
5. Upgrade product
6. Higher prices
7. Reduce manufacturing costs
8. Sub-contract production

Results
a. Cut unit costs
b. Job losses
c. Reduced sales
d. Market share increases
e. Cut profits
f. Unit costs come down
g. Higher profits
h. Adapt to market

2. PRESENTATION

In this extract from a meeting, **conditional** sentences were used to express **possible** results.
The construction used was:

Condition	Result
If we reduce prices	→ our market share will increase.
If we can reduce unit costs	→ that must put us in a strong position.

Note: The present simple is used in the **condition**.
The future with *will* or a modal in the present is used in the **result**.

We often reverse the sentence:

Result		Condition
But it'll mean job losses	◄──	if we sub-contract production.
Unit costs can only come down	◄──	if we invest in new plant.

3. CONTROLLED PRACTICE

Make conditional sentences from the prompts below. You must decide which is the condition and which is the result, and use an appropriate verb, where necessary.

e.g. Sales increase/good advertising campaign

Sales will increase if we have a good advertising campaign.
if there is a good advertising campaign.

1. More satisfied customers/improve the delivery service
   ....
2. Rationalise production/unit costs reduced
   ....
3. Job losses/rationalise production
   ....
4. Install robots/lower labour costs
   ....
5. Price war/competitors enter the market
   ....
6. Charge higher prices/upgrade the product
   ....
7. Earn larger profits/increase our margins
   ....

8. No research/no new products

   ....

9. Not offer better salaries/not attract the best people

   ....

10. Fewer meetings/more time to do the job

    ....

4. TRANSFER

Pair work
Student B: Turn to the Key section.
Student A:
1. Ask Student B 'What will happen if …?'
Conditions
   a. Your company moves to a new location?
   b. Your English improves a lot?
   c. You are offered a new job abroad?
   d. You win the lottery?

2. Now answer Student B's questions like this:
   If I get a promotion, I will …

WORD CHECK

strategy	plan of future action
to define	to find
flexible	can be changed
objective	something which you aim for
market share	percentage of a total market which the sales of a company or product cover
to reduce	to make less or smaller
margins	difference between the buying and selling price
long-term	for a long period of time
prospect	possibility for the future
to invest	to spend money usefully
plant	factory
manufacturing	production
to upgrade	to make better, to improve
competitive	difficult, as a result of the activities of other companies working in the same area
rapidly	quickly
to adapt	to change
to sub-contract	to agree with another company that they will do part of the work

Unit 16

Competition

Comparison of adjectives

1. LISTENING The Sales Manager of Brotherton Plc is talking about the company's main competitors. As you listen, complete the table below. Rank in order 1–4.

	Age in market (1 = oldest)	Market share (1 = biggest)	Product price (1 = cheapest)	Profitability (1 = most profitable)
Brotherton			2	
Benton	4	1		
Zecron				2
Mansell	1		4	

— 79 —

2. PRESENTATION

In this extract you heard a variety of comparative and superlative forms of adjectives.

2.1 Forming comparative and superlative adjectives
2.1.1 Adjectives with one syllable

long	long**er**	the long**est**
big	big**ger**	the big**gest**
low	low**er**	the low**est**
high	high**er**	the high**est**
late	lat**er**	the lat**est**

2.1.2 Two-syllable adjectives ending in *y*

heavy	heav**ier**	the heav**iest**
early	ear**lier**	the ear**liest**

2.1.3 Adjectives with two or more syllables

reliable	**more** reliable	**the most** reliable
expensive	**more** expensive	**the most** expensive
profitable	**more** profitable	**the most** profitable

2.2 Modifying comparative adjectives
We can also modify the strength of the comparative adjective.

- If we want to make it stronger, we can use **much**.
  e.g. a *much* smaller market share
  much more reliable

- If we want to make it weaker, we can use **slightly**.
  e.g. *slightly* higher prices
  slightly longer

3. CONTROLLED PRACTICE

Use the table in the Listening section and the language in the Presentation section to complete these sentences.

1. Mansell have been in the market _____ _____.
2. Brotherton entered the market _____ than Benton.
3. Benton entered the market ten years _____ than Brotherton.
4. Benton have _____ _____ market share.
5. Mansell have a much _____ market share than Brotherton.
6. Benton's products are sold at _____ _____ prices.
7. Mansell's products are sold at _____ _____ prices than Brotherton's.
8. Zecron's products are _____ _____ than Brotherton's.
9. Mansell is _____ _____ profitable company.
10. Brotherton is _____ _____ than Benton.

4. TRANSFER

Pair work
Student B: Turn to the Key section.
Student A:

1. Ask Student B questions so that you can complete the table below by inserting ranking figures (1–4). Ask questions like:

   Which is the most _____ company?

   Is _____ more _____ than _____ ?

Company	Turnover (1 = biggest)	Profitability (1 = most profitable)	Share capital (1 = largest)	Employees (1 = most)
Cittabank				
R and D Building Society				
Elton Bank				
Finance Banking				

2. Use the table below to answer Student B's questions. Answer like this:

   AG Oil is the most _modern_

   Natelcom is more _modern_ than _RAM_.

Company	Age in market (1 = oldest)	Technology (1 = most modern)	Premises (1 = largest)	Employees (1 = best trained)
A G Oil	3	1	3	1
Natelcom	1	2	4	3
RAM	4	3	1	2
Chand Chemicals	2	4	2	4

WORD CHECK

competition	trying to do better than another company
competitor	person or company who tries to do better than another person or company
competitive	difficult, as a result of competition
to enter the market	to start to do business
to grow	to become bigger
rapidly	quickly
market share	percentage of a total market which the sales of a company or product cover
attractive(ly)	in a way that looks good
weakness	position of not being strong or active
major	important, big
return	official report of income and profits
investment	money spent in order to make a profit in the future
plant	factory
to overtake	to pass
to achieve	to succeed in doing something
turnover	amount of sales
reliable	can be trusted
reputation	general opinion about something or someone
to hold on to	to keep

Unit 17

Project timing

Prepositions of time

1. LISTENING Listen to the telephone conversation about the timing of a construction project. As you listen, complete the key for the project planner below.

2. Presentation

Notice how the following prepositions are used to refer to time:

on	**days, dates**
	on 1 April, on Tuesday
	also
	on time = punctually
at	**precise times**
	at 6 o'clock, at 14.00
	at the beginning/end
	also
	at the weekend
	at night
in	**periods of time**
	in June, in 1987, in autumn, in the morning
	also
	in time = in sufficient time
by	**a deadline** (at the latest)
	It must be finished by 18.00

Notice also these expressions which are used when talking about timing:

The project { **is due to** / **is expected to** / **is scheduled to** } start on …

3. Controlled Practice

Complete these sentences with an appropriate preposition of time.

1. The work is due to begin _____ the end of April.
2. We are hoping to meet the engineer _____ the weekend.
3. We expect to sign the contract sometime _____ June.
4. We arrived _____ time to see them leave.
5. They are scheduled to finish _____ the middle of July.
6. I arranged to meet him _____ 15.30 _____ Tuesday.
7. The plane took off precisely _____ time.

8. We are busiest _____ spring.

9. The contract must be finalised _____ the end of the month, at the latest.

10. He phoned me _____ one o'clock _____ night.

4. TRANSFER

Pair work

Student B: Turn to the Key section.
Student A:
1. Ask Student B questions in order to complete the project planner. You should insert the stages/events listed in the Key.

Project Planner	January				February				March				April				KEY	
	3	10	17	24	31	7	14	21	28	7	14	21	28	4	11	18	25	▨ Preliminary study
																		X Contract negotiation
																		▥ Feasibility study
																		▮ Training
																		▨ Installation
																		O Implementation date

2. Think of a coming event in your own life, or in the news, in which a number of definite stages are involved. Describe this to Student B. Use sentences like:

We'll leave _____ at _____ o'clock.

The Prime Minister is expected to meet the President on _____.

WORD CHECK

construction	building
project	plan
pilot study	test which, if successful, will be expanded into a full operation
to last	to take time
contractor	person or company working according to a written agreement
to schedule	to plan the time when something will happen
to sign	to write one's name on a document to approve or accept it
contract	legal agreement between two parties
stage	step
excavation	work of making a hole by digging
to sub-contract	to arrange that another company will do part of the work
foundations	base of a building put deep into the ground to support the walls
tight (schedule)	leaving no extra time at all to put right mistakes or fix difficulties

Unit 18

Factory tour

Prepositions of place

1. LISTENING A Plant Manager is showing some visitors around an electronic assembly plant that makes printed circuit boards. As you listen, match each object with the phrase describing its location. The first one has been done for you.

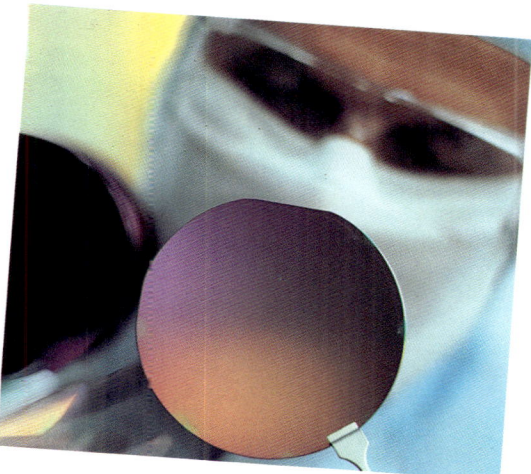

Supply area

Object
1. raw materials
2. conveyor
3. components
4. boards
5. chemicals

Location phrase
a. takes them into supply room
b. stacked against the wall
c. off-loaded onto a conveyor
d. stored between the boards and shelves
e. stored on shelves

Assembly area

Object
6. boards
7. holes
8. boards
9. components
10. boards

Location phrase
f. come out of drilling machine
g. inserted into boards
h. pass through a cutter
i. come off a conveyor
j. drilled into boards

Despatch area

Object
11. assembled boards
12. despatch area
13. boards
14. boards
15. boards

Location phrase
k. stacked in front of table
l. sorted on this table
m. go into despatch area
n. packed in boxes
o. behind this door

2. PRESENTATION

Notice how the following prepositions are used to refer to place:

to

at

from

onto

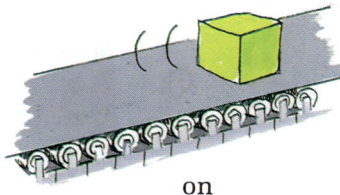
on

off

into

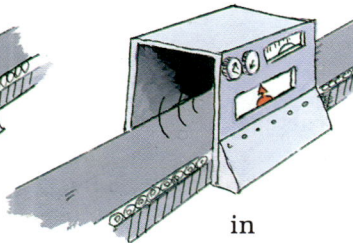
in

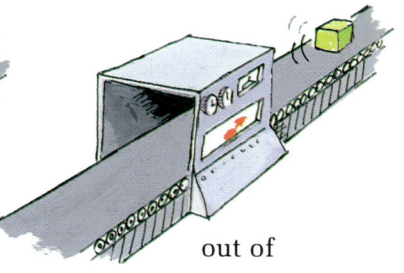
out of

above

below

in front of

behind

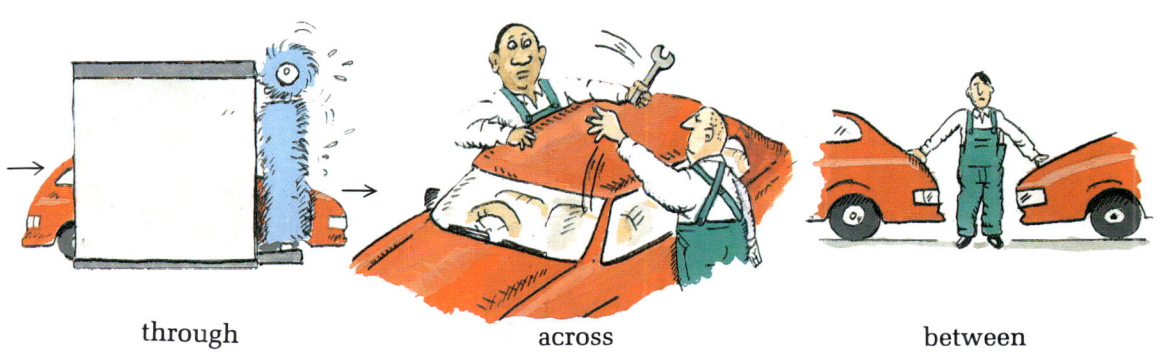

through   across   between

3. CONTROLLED PRACTICE

Complete the following sentences with an appropriate preposition.

1. London lies _____ the River Thames.
2. I'll meet you _____ the airport. (*i.e. the terminal building*)
3. I'll meet you _____ the airport. (*i.e. that point on the map*)
4. (*looking at a map*) I can't find Tweedale Street at all. It must be _____ the map.
5. Cologne is _____ Bonn and Düsseldorf.
6. We walked _____ the main hall to the conference room.
7. My car is parked _____ _____ the building.
8. Where's Peter? He just walked _____ _____ the office.
9. Come _____ my office. We can talk in private there.
10. On a clear day, you can see _____ the Channel _____ France.
11. Now I remember the bridge. It's _____ the River Avon.
12. Exhausted after the meeting, he dropped his briefcase _____ the desk.
13. He put the document _____ the safe.
14. I took the letter _____ _____ the filing cabinet.
15. The ship sails _____ Hamburg _____ Stockholm.
16. The tunnel will be built 100 metres _____ sea level.

4. Transfer

Pair work
Student B: Turn to the Key section.
Student A:
1. Complete the plan of the office to show where the following items of furniture are. Student B will tell you where they should be.

safe   book shelves   fax machine   photocopier   filing cabinet

2. Now use your completed plan to tell Student B where the rest of the furniture is located.

3. When you have finished, compare your plan with Student B's. They should look the same.

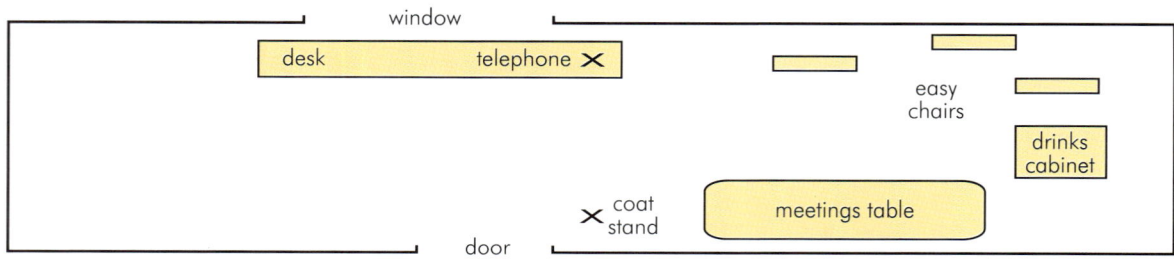

WORD CHECK

plant	factory
supply area	place where goods come before assembly
assembly area	place where items are put together from various parts
despatch area	place from which assembled items are sent to customers
raw materials	basic materials used to make finished products
truck	large motor vehicle for carrying goods
conveyor	moving belt for transport of products
storage	keeping in store
shelf	flat surface attached to a wall on which items can be placed
component	part which will be put into a final product
to stack up	to put things on top of each other
board	long, thin, flat piece of solid material, e.g. wood
process	step or steps involved in manufacturing products in factories
shape	form, appearance
cutter	instrument for cutting
to drill	to make a hole or holes with a tool
to insert	to put in
to sort	to put in order according to size, etc.
to pack	to put things into a container for sending or selling

Unit 19

Market research

Question formation

1. LISTENING A market researcher asks a consumer questions. Listen and fill in the questionnaire.

Quest Market Research
Consumer Survey

Name _____
Address _____
Telephone _____
Accommodation   Own home ☐   Rent ☐
                 Hotel ☐   Other ...... ☐
Number in home ☐
Place of work: Husband *Courtaulds*
               Wife _____
Place of study: Child 1 _____
                Child 2 *Independent Boys' School*
Holidays per year
Location _____
                              abroad
        autumn _____

Money spent on last summer holiday _____
Location of last holiday _____

2. PRESENTATION

The market researcher used two different types of question:

- Direct questions
- Statement questions

Now look at the formation of these questions.

2.1 Direct questions
2.1.1 Wh-questions

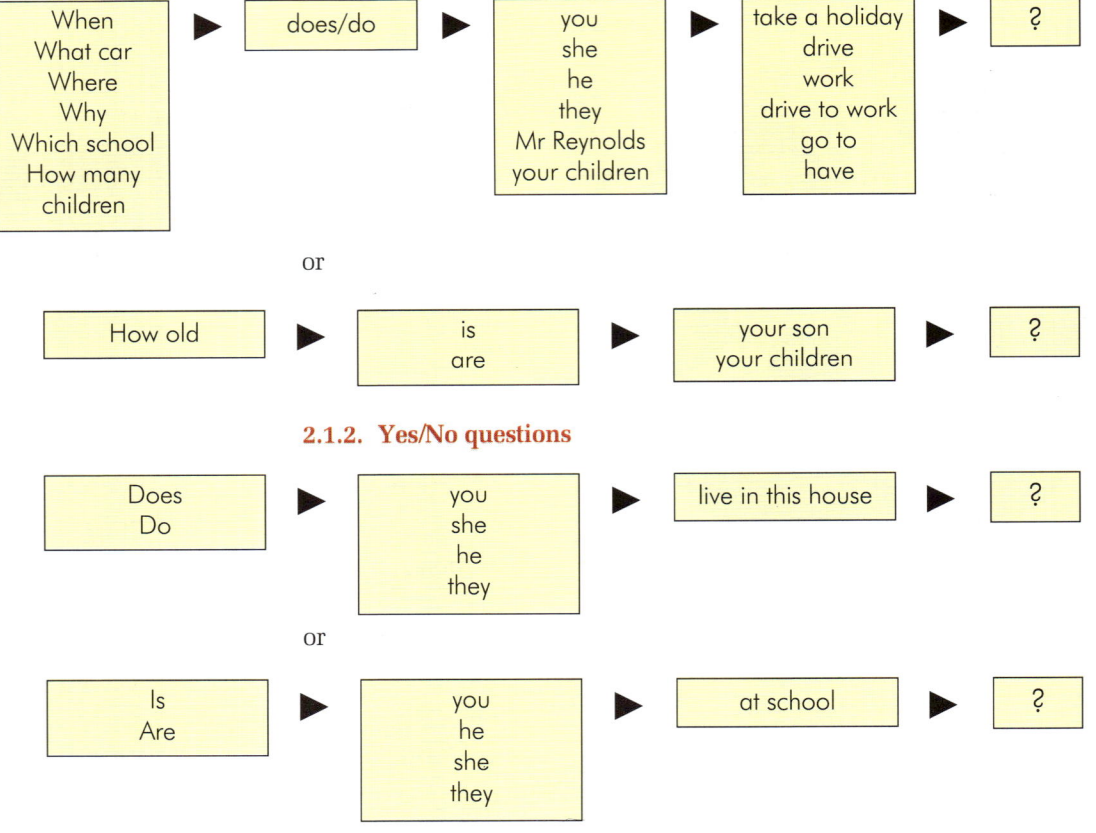

2.1.2. Yes/No questions

2.2 Statement questions

These are often used for *checking* information:

It's Mr and Mrs J. Reynolds, isn't it?
The address is 21 Pine Avenue? (*rising intonation*)
Your telephone number is 56822, is that right?

3. CONTROLLED PRACTICE

You are doing a market research survey. You are interviewing a man called Mr P. Thomson. Ask questions as follows:

1. Check that his name is P. Thomson.
   .... ?

2. Check that his address is 45 Main Street.
   .... ?

3. Check that he owns his house.
   .... ?

4. Ask where he works.
   .... ?

5. Ask if he has worked there for long.
   .... ?

6. Ask how he travels to work.
   .... ?

7. Ask if he has any children.
   .... ?

8. Ask how old they are.
   .... ?

9. Ask if they are at school.
   .... ?

10. Ask what they do in the evenings.
   ....?

11. Ask how often he goes to the cinema.
   ....?

12. Ask if he ever goes to restaurants.
   ....?

13. Ask when he goes to bed.
   ....?

4. Transfer

Group work

You are the marketing team of a company which manufactures soap and hair shampoo. Your task is to design a questionnaire to find out what ideas consumers have for a new shampoo. Your questionnaire should:

- be aimed at shoppers in supermarkets
- not take more than three minutes to answer.

First decide what information you want to collect.
Then design the questionnaire.
Finally, try your questionnaire on other members of your class.

WORD CHECK

market researcher	person who examines the possible sales of a product before it is put on the market
consumer	person who buys and uses goods and services
personal	private
to own	to have, to possess
roughly	about, approximately
firm	company
abroad	in/to another country
to suppose	to estimate
actually	in fact

Unit 20

The budget meeting

Modals

1. LISTENING Listen to the extract from a budget meeting. Peter, John and Susan are discussing next year's departmental budgets. As you listen, indicate their opinions in the table below. Use these symbols:

+ = more money should be spent
– = less money should be spent
OK = the proposed figure should remain the same

Budget proposals

Department	Budget	Peter	John	Susan
Research	£25,000			
Marketing	£45,000			
Production	£145,000			
Sales	£55,000			

2. PRESENTATION

Modal verbs (such as *should*, *ought*, *can*, *could*, *might*) can be used to indicate speakers' attitudes or opinions. These can be categorised as follows:

- strong recommendation
- possibility
- slight possibility
- impossibility

Now look at the modals used to express opinions in the meeting and notice how the *strength* of the opinion can be varied by using these modal verbs.

2.1 Strong recommendation
We **should** increase the research budget.
The figure **shouldn't** be changed.
Production **ought** to manage with less.

2.2 Possibility
We **could** reduce the figure for marketing.

2.3 Slight possibility
We **might** save a bit on after-sales.

2.4 Impossibility
We **can't** cut the production budget.

3. CONTROLLED PRACTICE

Use the language in the Presentation section to transform the sentences. The first one has been done for you.

1. I strongly recommend we reduce the sales budget.

   We should/ought to reduce the sales budget.

2. There's a small chance that marketing would accept a cut in their budget.

   Marketing ....

3. A cut in the production budget is out of the question.

   We ....

4. It's possible to spend more on direct sales activities.

   We ....

5. It is advisable to reduce the total budget.

   We ....

6. It's impossible for research to continue on this budget.

   Research ....

7. There is a possibility that more money will be made available.

   More money ....

8. I strongly recommend we do not cut the marketing budget.

   We ....

9. There's a small chance sales will not reach their target.

   Sales ....

10. Production will possibly need more money later in the year.

    Production ....

4. TRANSFER

Group work

What do you think? Give your opinions on the following statements.

1. Governments should stop spending money on space research.
2. Everyone should learn how to use a computer.
3. Everyone should try to gain overseas experience in their job.
4. We should do more to conserve (save) energy.
5. All companies should run staff training schemes.

Here is an example of a group discussion to start you off.

A: I think governments should stop spending money on space research.

B: I agree. They ought to spend the money on more useful things, like helping the poor or improving hospitals.

C: But a lot of good, useful products have come out of space research.

D: That's right. Without space research, hospitals might not have some of the advanced medical equipment they have now.

A: But we could spend the money on medical research instead of space research and have even better, even more up-to-date equipment.

WORD CHECK

budget	plan of expected spending and income
opinion	idea
to propose	to suggest
proposal	suggestion
to reduce	to make less or smaller
to allow	to make it possible for someone to do something
to increase	to make more or bigger
launch	act of putting a new product on the market
mid-year	in the middle of the year
to cut	to reduce
investment	money usefully spent
to save	not to spend money
after-sales (service)	service of a machine carried out by the seller for some time after the machine has been bought
out of the question	not for discussion, unacceptable

– KEY –

KEY Unit 1

1. LISTENING   Tapescript

In this unit you will hear a number of people introducing themselves.

1. A: Hello, let me introduce myself. My name's Klein, Günther Klein.
   B: Pleased to meet you. I'm Geoff Snowdon.

2. A: How do you do? My name's Paul Matthews.
   B: Nice to meet you. Mine's Akira Mishima.

3. A: Hello, I'm Tom.
   B: Nice to meet you. My name's Francine.

4. A: Peter, could you introduce me to the Marketing Manager?
   B: Of course, John … Philip, let me introduce you to John, our new Computer Manager.
   C: Nice to meet you, John, we're going to be working together.

5. A: Herr Tübingen, I haven't met your Managing Director yet.
   B: Oh, I'm sorry. Come and meet him. Dr Mannheim, this is Mr Roberts. He's over from the States on a visit.
   C: Very nice to meet you, Mr Roberts. How long are you here for?

6. A: Jane, I don't know anyone here. You'll have to introduce me.
   B: Of course, I'll introduce you to Roger first. He's the host … Roger, this is Susan. She's just moved to the area.
   C: Nice to meet you, Susan. Do you come from these parts?

7. A: Let me introduce you two. Maxine, this is Francis.
   B: Nice to meet you, Maxine. Are you an old friend of Tony's?
   C: Oh yes, Tony and I have known each other for years, haven't we?
   A: Yes, that's right.

Answers to the listening task
a. 3   b. 1   c. 6   d. 2   e. 5   f. 7   g. 4

Answers to the Presentation listening task
Introduction 1 *(F)*   Introduction 5 *(F)*
Introduction 2 *(F)*   Introduction 6 *(I)*
Introduction 3 *(I)*   Introduction 7 *(I)*
Introduction 4 *(I)*

3. CONTROLLED PRACTICE

1. Peter King: Hello, *let me introduce myself*. My name's Peter King.
   Jack Simpson: *Nice/Pleased to meet you*. I'm Jack Simpson.

2. Sarah: Philip, *I don't know anyone* here. You'll have to *introduce me*.
   Philip: Of *course*, I'll *introduce you* to James. He's an old friend of mine. James, *this is* Sarah, she's just joined the company.
   James: *(Very) nice to meet you*, Sarah. Where do you come from?

3. Pete: Rod, *I haven't met* Mrs Rogers, the Purchasing Manager from Kentons.
   Rod: I'm *sorry*. Come and meet her. Mrs Rogers, *let me introduce you to* Pete Taylor, our Export Sales Manager.
   Mrs Rogers: *(Very) nice to meet you*. What countries do you cover?

4. Klaus Fischer: How *do you do?* My name's *Klaus Fischer*.
   American: *Pleased/Nice to meet you. Mine's* Brenda Cole.

KEY Unit 2

1. LISTENING Tapescript

In this unit you will hear three dialogues. In each dialogue two people introduce and present themselves and others.

Dialogue 1

A: Nice to meet you, Peter. What do you do for a living?

B: I'm in computers – software development. What about you, John?

A: Oh, I work for Manders – in the Personnel Department. Not a bad job.

B: Is that one of your colleagues over there?

A: Yes, that's Susan. She works in the Accounts Department. Let me introduce you.

Dialogue 2

A: Hello, I'm Mike.

B: Nice to meet you, I'm Sarah. I haven't seen you around before.

A: No, I've just started work for Manders. I'm in the Sales Department.

B: What do you do there?

A: Oh, I'm on the market research side. And you?

B: Well, I've been with Manders for years. I'm Mr Field's Personal Assistant. He's the Sales Director.

A: Ah, I haven't met him. Is he here?

B: Yes, that's him. Let me introduce you.

Dialogue 3

A: That's interesting. Do you work here, Martin?

B: Yes, I'm in Finance. What about you, Jean?

A: Well, my husband works at Manders. He's in the Production Department.

B: Oh yes, I think I've met him. What about you? Do you work?

A: Yes, I'm a fashion designer. I work from home.

B: That's interesting.

Answers to the listening task

1. c   4. d   7. i
2. f   5. b   8. e
3. g   6. h   9. a

3. CONTROLLED PRACTICE

A.
1. What do you do *for* a living?
2. I work *for/with/at* Manders.
3. I'm *on* the recruitment side.
4. He's *in* the Production Department.
5. I work *from/at* home.
6. She's been *with/at* Manders *for* years.

B.
1. b. Well, I work in Sales.
2. c. Oh, I haven't met him.
3. b. I live right here.
4. c. Oh yes, I think I've met him.
5. c. No, I'm new here.

KEY – Unit 2

4. TRANSFER   Pair work

Student B: Below are three business cards. Use the information to practise three introductory conversations about jobs and places of work.

Futura SOFTware Ltd

Julia Hampton *Managing Director*

23 Darlinghurst Rd, Sidney 2010
Telephone 2 357 4820 – Fax 2 357 2987

Manders INTERNATIONAL Plc

Kim Malcolm
Sales Director

25 Salisbury Drive, London SW1
Tel: 071 456-6550
Fax: 071 456-9234

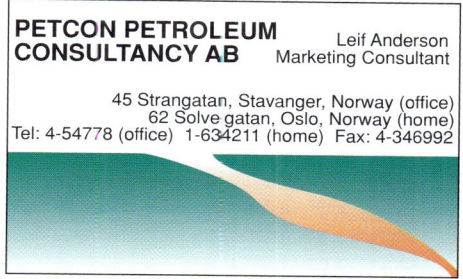

PETCON PETROLEUM CONSULTANCY AB   Leif Anderson
Marketing Consultant

45 Strangatan, Stavanger, Norway (office)
62 Solve gatan, Oslo, Norway (home)
Tel: 4-54778 (office) 1-634211 (home) Fax: 4-346992

KEY Unit 3

1. LISTENING   Tapescript

In this unit you will hear five dialogues. In each dialogue the speakers are strangers and are trying to find points of common interest.

Dialogue 1

A: Is this your first trip to Japan?

B: Yes, it is.

A: Do you like it here?

B: Yes, it seems interesting.

A: Would you like another drink?

B: Thank you.

Dialogue 2

A: How was your trip?

B: Fine, thanks.

A: How do you find Tokyo?

B: Very interesting.

A: Which hotel are you staying in?

B: The Sheraton.

— 103 —

KEY – Unit 3

Dialogue 3

A: Is this your first trip to Japan?

B: Yes, but hopefully not my last.

A: I'm pleased to hear that. Have you found time to see much?

B: Well, I visited the gardens.

A: Oh, are you interested in gardens?

B: Actually, yes, it's my hobby.

A: Mine too …

Dialogue 4

A: Are you staying long?

B: No, unfortunately only a couple of weeks.

A: Business or pleasure?

B: Business, I'm afraid. My company is setting up an office here in Tokyo.

A: Really? Where is your company based?

B: In Detroit, sort of north mid-west of the States.

A: Yes, I know it. I visited it two years ago.

B: Ah, really? …

Dialogue 5

A: I believe you're in fashion.

B: Yes that's right – on the design side.

A: That's a coincidence. My wife's a fashion designer.

B: Oh, I'd like to meet her.

A: You must come round to dinner one evening.

B: That would be nice.

A: Good, I'll fix it up later this week.

Answers to the listening task

	Successful (✔)	Unsuccessful (✘)
Dialogue 1		✘
Dialogue 2		✘
Dialogue 3	✔	
Dialogue 4	✔	
Dialogue 5	✔	

Dialogue 1: No

Dialogue 2: Sheraton

Dialogue 3: Gardens

Dialogue 4: Detroit

Dialogue 5: Fashion

3. CONTROLLED PRACTICE

Dialogue 1

Is this your first trip over here?

No, I've been to the States before, but this is the first time in Atlanta.

So, what do you think of Atlanta?

Well, it's not what I expected.

Really? What did you expect?

Well, I suppose I thought it would be more traditional.

There is a part like that. You must let me show you around.

That would be interesting.

Fine, I'll see what I can arrange.

KEY – Unit 3

Dialogue 2

Are you staying long?

No, just a couple of days.

That's a pity. There's a lot to see.

I'm sure. I hope to get back here again.

Good. Are you here on business then?

Yes, we're thinking of setting up an office here.

Really? That's interesting. What line are you in?

Dialogue 3

I believe you're in journalism.

Yes, that's right – on the editorial side.

That's interesting. My son is an editor on the local paper.

Really? I expect I'll meet him.

Yes, what about coming round for a drink? I could introduce you to him.

That would be nice.

Dialogue 4

How do you find the weather here?

A bit warmer than back home.

Oh, so where do you come from?

Scotland. This time of year it's pretty cold.

I can imagine. I've never been but people tell me it's very beautiful.

Yes, that's right. The best time to visit is in the summer.

Maybe I'll get across next year.

Well, if you do come across, you must visit us.

KEY Unit 4

1. LISTENING   Tapescript

In the first part of this unit you will hear fifteen exchanges. In each exchange there is a statement or question by one person followed by a response by another person.

1. Thanks for the lovely evening.
   → Glad you enjoyed it.
2. How about a drink?
   → Don't mention it.
3. Do you mind if I smoke?
   → Yes, I do.
4. Could you hand me that pen?
   → Of course. Here you are.
5. My father died last night.
   → Oh, I am sorry to hear that.
6. Have a good weekend.
   → So do I.
7. Thanks for your help.
   → Never mind.
8. I'm sorry, I must have got the wrong number.
   → It doesn't matter.
9. Best of luck in your new job.
   → Not at all.

KEY – Unit 4

10. He's 95, you know!
    → Really?
11. I think we should leave now.
    → So do I.
12. We've had a very good year.
    → I'm glad to hear that.
13. Can I ask you a question?
    → Don't mention it.
14. Would you like to go to a concert this evening?
    → Yes, I'd love to.
15. I didn't get the job.
    → That's true.

Answers to the listening task

1. ✔	6. ✘	11. ✔
2. ✘	7. ✘	12. ✔
3. ✘	8. ✔	13. ✘
4. ✔	9. ✘	14. ✔
5. ✔	10. ✔	15. ✘

Appropriate responses

1. Thanks for the lovely evening
   → Glad you enjoyed it.
2. How about a drink?
   → That would be nice.
3. Do you mind if I smoke?
   → No, of course not.
4. Could you hand me that pen?
   → Of course. Here you are.
5. My father died last night.
   → Oh, I am sorry to hear that.
6. Have a good weekend.
   → You too.
7. Thanks for your help.
   → You're welcome.
8. I'm sorry, I must have got the wrong number.
   → It doesn't matter.
9. Best of luck in your new job.
   → Thanks very much.
10. He's 95, you know!
    → Really?
11. I think we should leave now.
    → So do I.
12. We've had a very good year.
    → I'm glad to hear that.
13. Can I ask you a question?
    → Yes, of course.
14. Would you like to go to a concert this evening?
    → Yes, I'd love to.
15. I didn't get the job.
    → Never mind. Better luck next time.

3. CONTROLLED PRACTICE

(Note: There are other appropriate answers.)

1. Never mind. Better luck next time.
2. No, of course not.
3. Yes, I'd love/like to.
4. It doesn't matter/Don't worry/Never mind.
5. Of course. Here you are.
6. So do I/Me too/I hope so too.
7. You too/Same to you.
8. Really?
9. Me too/So do I/I think so too.
10. Glad you liked/enjoyed it.
11. I am sorry to hear that/Hard luck.
12. Yes, of course/Certainly.
13. That would be nice/That's a good idea.
14. I'd love/like to.
15. Don't worry/Never mind/It doesn't matter.

KEY Unit 5

1. LISTENING Tapescript

In this unit you will hear a presentation of the organisation of a company called Rossomon Plc.

I'd like to say a few words about the organisational structure of Rossomon. Now, if you look at the transparency you will see that the Managing Director, that is Mr Bunce, is responsible for running the company and is accountable to the Board.

Now, he is assisted by four executive departments. These are Human Resources, which is responsible for personnel, training and management development; then there is the Finance Department which takes care of corporate finance and accounting; next, we have the Management Services Department, led by Peter Jenkins who is in charge of rationalisation throughout the company; and finally there is the R & D Department – research and development – which works closely with the five regions on new product development.

So this then brings me on to the regions. Directly under the Managing Director there are five Regional Managers. Each of them is responsible for the day-to-day management of a territory – these are geographically split into North, South, East, West, and Central Regions.

Now then, the five regions are supported by two sections – Marketing and Technical Services. They are organised on a matrix basis with section leaders accountable to the Regional Managers. They work closely with the regions on the marketing and technical side.

Now, in addition to the parent company, Rossomon has three subsidiaries, namely Rossomon France, Germany and Japan. The subsidiaries report to the Export Sales Department, which in turn is accountable to the Board.

Right, well that's a brief overview. Are there any questions?

Answers to the listening task

1. Managing Director
2. Finance Department
3. Management Services Department
4. Research and Development Department
5. Regional Managers
6. South
7. East
8. Central
9. Technical Services Section
10. Rossomon Germany
11. Export Sales Department

3. CONTROLLED PRACTICE

1. The Managing Director *reports/is accountable* to the Board.
2. The Managing Director *is responsible* for running the company.
3. The Managing Director *is supported/is assisted* by four executive departments.
4. *Under* the Managing Director, there are five regional divisions.
5. Each Regional Manager is *in charge* of a territory.
6. The five regions *are supported/are assisted* by two other sections – Marketing and Technical Services.
7. The Section Leaders *report/are accountable* to the Regional Managers.
8. In addition to the *parent* company, Rossomon has three *subsidiaries*.

KEY – Unit 5

9. The subsidiaries *consist of* Rossomon France, Rossomon Germany and Rossomon Japan.
10. The subsidiaries *report/are accountable* to the Export Sales Department.

4. TRANSFER   Pair work

1. **Student B**: Listen to Student A's description of the typical management structure of a British company. Use the information to complete the organisation chart for Semling Photographics Plc.

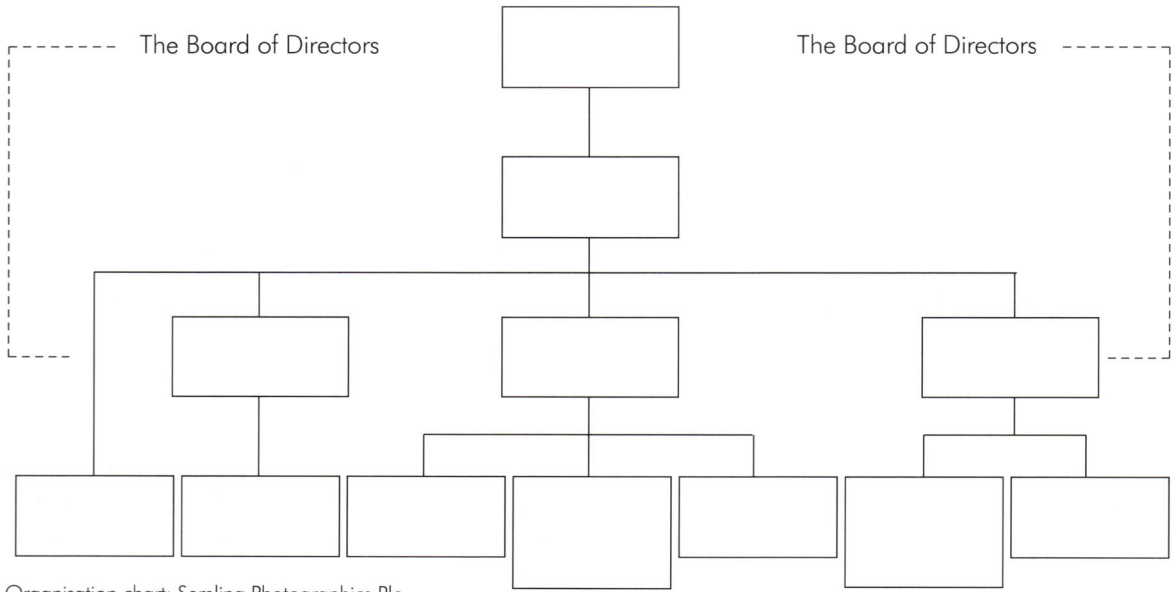

Organisation chart: Semling Photographics Plc

KEY – Unit 5

2. **Student B**: Now describe the management structure of a more typical American company to Student A. Use the organisation chart for Felton Computers.

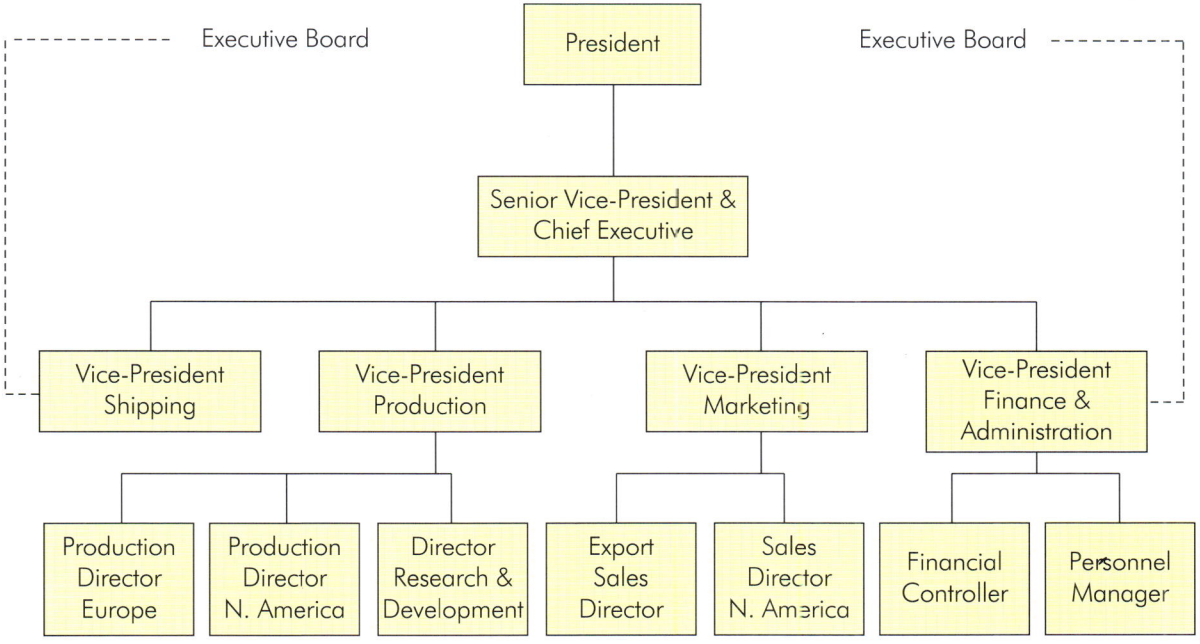

Organisation chart: Felton Computers

KEY Unit 6

1. LISTENING   Tapescript

In this unit you will hear a phone call about the supply of office shelving systems.

A: Good morning. I'm phoning to enquire about your office shelving system ... code number SS007.

B: Oh yes, what would you like to know?

A: Well, I'd like to check on the dimensions first – make sure that they'll fit. First of all, how wide are they?

B: Just a moment, sir, I'll get the specifications ... you asked about the width ... yes, the standard unit is 3.5 metres wide.

KEY – Unit 6

A: And the height?

B: They're 2 metres high with flexible positions for the shelves.

A: How many shelves can actually be fitted?

B: Really as many as you like, but normally five.

A: I see. I need to know how much they stick out – in other words, how deep are they?

B: They're 30 centimetres deep.

A: Thanks, that's the dimensions. Now, what about delivery?

B: Well, it depends how far you are from our warehouse.

A: We're about ten miles from the centre.

B: I see – well, that's in our free delivery area, so there'll be no extra charge for delivery.

A: Good. Actually, what I meant was how long does it take after I place an order?

B: I see, sir. We guarantee delivery within two weeks.

A: Good. Well, we're interested in ten of your standard units for a suite of offices. How much do you charge?

B: Well, the unit cost is £98 but in view of the size of the order, we can offer a 5 per cent discount … just a moment, I'll just do the figures … yes, that comes to £931 – let's round it off and call it £930.

A: That sounds reasonable. Finally, what sort of guarantee do you offer?

B: Well, these units are extremely sturdy and reliable. There's the usual one-year guarantee but they have an average life of at least 20 years …

Answers to the listening task

Dimensions:	Width	3.5 m
	Height	2.0 m
	Depth	30 cm
Delivery:	Cost	No charge
	Time	Two weeks
Price:	Unit price	£98
	Discount price	£930 for 10 units
Guarantee period:		One year
Average life:		At least 20 years

3. CONTROLLED PRACTICE

A.

Noun form	Adjective	Opposite adjective
width	wide	narrow
length	long	short
depth	deep	shallow
height	high	low
distance	far	near
speed	fast	slow
reliability	reliable	unreliable

B.

1. How wide is it?
2. How deep is it?
3. How fast is it?
4. How long does it take to deliver?
5. How much is it/does it cost/do you charge to deliver?
6. How reliable is it?
7. How long is the cable?
8. How long is the guarantee (period)?
9. How much does it cost/is it?
10. How far is (it to) the nearest service centre?

KEY – Unit 6

4. Transfer   Pair work

Student B: Student A is going to ask you about the personal computer below. Answer the questions about the product features according to the information on the specification sheet.

Dimensions
Width .... 29 cm
Height .... 6 cm
Depth .... 24 cm

Delivery
Cost .... no charge
Time .... 7 days

Price
For one £1,200.00
For more than 5 .. £1,000.00 each

Guarantee period ....

KEY Unit 7

1. LISTENING   Tapescript

In this unit you will hear three telephone calls. In each call, the caller wants to make an arrangement.

Call 1

A: Krondike Electronics. Can I help you?

B: Yes, I'd like to speak to Mr Edwards, please.

A: Who's calling, please?

B: John Bird.

A: Just a moment, Mr Bird; I'll put you through.

C: Miss Taylor speaking.

B: John Bird here. Can I speak to Mr Edwards?

C: I'm afraid he's out at the moment. Can I take a message?

B: Yes, could you ask him to call me back as soon as possible?

C: Yes, of course. Could I have your number?

B: He's got it, but just in case, it's 071-253 4686.

C: 071-253 4686. Thank you, Mr Bird. I'll make sure he gets the message.

B: Thank you. Bye.

C: Goodbye.

Call 2

A: John Bird speaking.

B: This is Pete Edwards. My secretary said you called.

A: Yes, that's right. Thanks for getting back. Look, the reason I called was we're having installation problems with the E 258.

B: Really? That surprises me. What sort of problems?

A: Well, it's a bit complicated. Could you send a technician round?

B: Of course, I'll get one round this afternoon.

A: That would be great.

B: OK, I'm sure we'll sort it out in no time. Bye.

A: Goodbye.

Call 3

A: Pearson and Brown. Can I help you?

B: This is Gerald Smith from Taylor & Sons. Could I speak to Mrs Phillips?

A: Just a moment, Mr Smith, I'll put you through.

C: Susan Phillips speaking.

B: Hello, Susan. This is Gerald Smith.

C: Oh hello, Gerald. How are you?

B: Fine. I'm just phoning to see if we could fix a meeting for next week.

C: Yes, of course. We've got to discuss next year's order. Just a moment, I'll get my diary ... Right, next week ... ?

B: Could you manage Tuesday?

C: I'm sorry. I'm out all day on Tuesday.

B: What about Friday then?

C: Yes, Friday in the morning would suit me fine.

B: Good, that suits me too. Shall we say 10 o'clock?

C: Fine. So 10 o'clock here then?

B: Yes, that's probably easiest. Right, I look forward to seeing you.

C: Bye.

B: Bye.

KEY – Unit 7

Answers to the listening task

Call	Name of person called	Name of caller	Reason for call	Result of call
1	Mr Edwards	John Bird	Installation problems	Edwards to call Bird back
2	John Bird	Pete Edwards	Returning call	Technician to go round in the afternoon
3	Susan Phillips	Gerald Smith	To fix a meeting	Meeting arranged 10.00 next Friday

3. CONTROLLED PRACTICE

A.

1. Pan Electronics. Can I help you?
   Yes, I'd like to speak to Miss Rathbone.
   Who's calling, please?
   Peter Jones.
   Just a moment, Mr Jones, I'll put you through.

2. Mr Gottman here. Could I speak to Mrs Fields?
   I'm afraid she's out at the moment. Can I take a message?
   Yes, could you ask her to call me back?
   Yes, of course. Could I have your number?
   She's got it, but just in case, it's 071-253 4686.

3. Just a moment, I'll get my diary ... you said next week?
   Yes, could you manage Wednesday?
   I'm sorry, I'm out on Wednesday.
   What about Thursday then?
   Yes, Thursday morning would suit me fine.
   Good, that suits me too. Shall we say 11 o'clock?

B.

1. c. Hello, John. I'm glad you called.
2. b. Yes, could you ask him to call me back?
3. b. Really? That surprises me.
4. c. I'm afraid I can't.
5. b. Right, I look forward to seeing you then.

4. TRANSFER   Pair work

Student B:

1. You are B Rogers' secretary. B Rogers is out. You will receive a call from Student A. Take a message. Make sure you get his/her name and telephone number.

2. You are B Rogers. Call Student A back. He/She will want to know the discount price for 10 pairs of model A293 shoes:
   Normal price: £39.00
   Discount on 10 pairs: 10%.

3. You are B Dunn (you can use the title Mr/Mrs/Miss/Ms or a first name). Student A will call you to arrange a meeting next week. Below is your diary for next week.

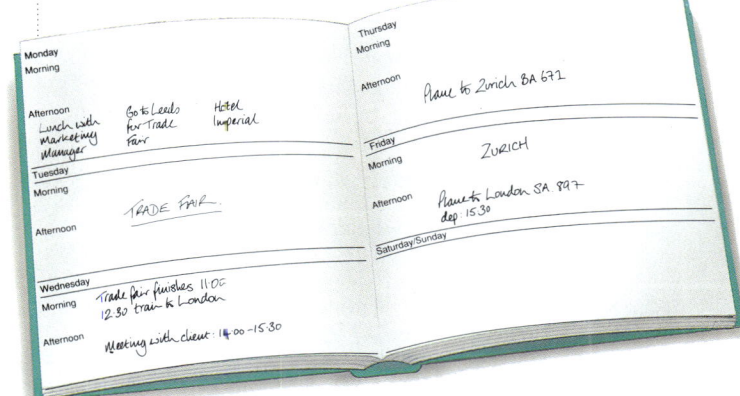

KEY Unit 8

1. LISTENING   Tapescript

In this unit you will hear a telephone call. The caller wants to make an appointment and needs to be sure that all the necessary information is correct.

A: Priority Investments. Can I help you?

B: Yes, this is George Biederbeke. Could I speak to someone in your corporate finance department?

A: Just a moment, I'll put you through.

C: Daniels speaking.

B: My name is George Biederbeke from the Austin Corporation. I'd like to make an appointment to see your Corporate Finance Manager.

C: Yes. Could you tell me what exactly you want to talk about?

B: Well, we're approaching a number of investment companies with a view to placing business with them.

C: I'm sorry, I didn't quite catch that.

B: I said that we are interested in your investment services.

C: I see, and you would like to meet our Corporate Finance Manager?

B: That's right.

C: When would be convenient for you?

B: Friday 28 June would suit me – in the afternoon.

C: Just a moment, I'll check with Mr Foster – our Corporate Finance Manager.

B: I'm sorry, I didn't catch his name.

C: Foster.

B: Right.

C: Just a moment, let me check … Yes, that'll be fine, about 2 p.m. Could I have your name again?

B: Biederbeke.

C: Could you spell that please?

B: B, I, E, D, E, R, B, E, K, E.

C: Right, I've got that. We'd like to send you a copy of our current prospectus. If you give me your address …

B: Of course. It's the Austin Corporation, 514 Seaview …

C: 514 Seanew.

B: No, it's Sea – *view*.

C: Right, I've got that.

B: 2952 Seattle.

C: 2952 Seattle. Right, let me just repeat that. Mr Biederbeke, Austin Corporation, 514 Seaview, 2952 Seattle.

B: Right.

C: And your telephone number, Mr Biederbeke?

B: It's (0452) 67791.

C: (0452) 67791. Right. We'll get the prospectus in the post to you today.

B: Good. Let me just confirm the appointment. Friday 28 June at 2 o'clock.

C: Fine, we look forward to seeing you then.

B: Goodbye.

C: Goodbye.

KEY – Unit 8

Answers to the listening task

First listening: Caller's notes

Name of company: *Priority Investments*

Name of Corporate Finance Manager: *Mr Foster*

Date of appointment: *Friday 28 June*

Time of appointment: *14.00*

Second listening: Called person's notes

Caller's name: *Mr Biederbeke*

Caller's company: *Austin Corporation*

Caller's address: *514 Seaview, 2952 Seattle*

Tel. no.: *(0452) 67791*

Reason for call: *Meeting with Mr Foster to discuss investment services*

Date of appointment: *Friday 28 June*

Time of appointment: *14.00*

Action: *1. Confirm appointment with Mr Foster.*
2. Send prospectus to Mr Biederbeke.

3. CONTROLLED PRACTICE

(Note: There are other appropriate answers.)

A.

1. A: My name's Pinkerton.
   B: *Could you spell that please?*
   A: Yes, it's P, I, N, K, E, R, T, O, N.

2. A: The address is 24 Tunnyside Lane.
   B: *Could you repeat that?*
   A: Yes, of course. 24 Tunnyside Lane.

3. A: My phone number is 0432 5686.
   B: 0432 5688?
   A: *No, it's 5686.*
   B: *Let me just repeat that – 0432 5686.*
   A: *That's right.*

4. A: I'd like an appointment with Mr Dunn.
   B: *Could you tell me exactly what* you would like to discuss?
   A: Yes, I'd like to talk about extending my credit.

5. A: We would like to visit your factory with a view to buying it.
   B: *I see.* When would you like to come?

6. A: The figure is 3.56 m.
   B: *I've got that.* And what was the other figure?

7. A: So, an appointment at two would suit you. *Could I have your name* again, please?
   B: Yes, certainly, it's Macintosh.
   A: *Could you spell that?*
   B: Yes, M, A, C, I, N, T, O, S, H.

B.

1. 0232–77551
2. 010–35–444–7889
3. 081–674–5500
4. 00–44–904–24246
5. 1–775–9191
6. 010–49–214–30761

4. TRANSFER   Pair work

Student B:

1. You work for Newsome Sports. Student A is going to phone you and place an order. Fill in the invoice below. Some of it has been done for you. When you have finished, give your customer the order number.

2. You are M Sanders (you can use the title Mr/Mrs/Miss/Ms or a first name). You work for Fenella Fashions. Their address is 193 Foxtown Street, Brighton BN25 4TS. Their phone number is 0273 474 222.

KEY – Unit 8

Phone SkiWear Plus. Ask the price of the following items and then place an order. Tell them you want to pay for the order 60 days after delivery and that you want the order delivered by the end of the month.

50 white ski hats
25 green ski hats
20 pairs leather ski gloves
Cost: 1 white ski hat ....

      1 green ski hat ....

      1 pair leather ski gloves ....

Order number ....

Newsome Sports Ltd
25 Margate Hill
London NW11 5SL

Tel: 081 745 638

VAT Registration 166 8653 17

Order No. A:946321

Description	Unit price	Quantity	Price
Training shoes	£39.00		£1950
Socks	£2.00		
Greys squash rackets	£48.00		

Total price £2490

Delivery date _____   Delivery to: _____
                                                  Contact person

Name of company _____   Phone _____

Number _____ Street _____

Town _____   Post Code _____

KEY Unit 9

1. LISTENING   Tapescript

In this unit you will hear an interview between a journalist and a businessman. The journalist is collecting information for an article about the businessman.

PJ: Oh, I usually get up about five, go for a jog before breakfast. We usually have breakfast around 6.30. Then I have time to read the papers.

J: Which papers do you take?

PJ: Well, *The Financial Times*, *The Times* and *The Independent*. I don't exactly read them from cover to cover.

J: No, of course not.

PJ: Well, after the papers, I leave for the office. I'm usually behind my desk by 7.30. The first job of the day is the post. My secretary sorts out those letters which need immediate attention. Then round about 9.00, I have a daily meeting with Pete Sykes, he's my deputy. We run through the agenda for the day.

J: What's a typical day like?

PJ: Well, there's no such thing as a typical day, but I have regular morning meetings with my Finance and Sales Directors. Of course, I travel abroad a lot, then I keep up-to-date by telephone.

J: What about lunch?

PJ: Well, I try to have lunch in the company canteen as often as possible. But, of course, sometimes I have lunch out with customers or the bank manager. People like that.

J: What about the afternoons?

PJ: If I'm in the country, I often go down to our plant and see how things are going. We have weekly management committee meetings on Friday afternoon. Then, of course, there are monthly board meetings, usually the first Monday of the month.

J: When do you finish work?

PJ: Round about seven. Then, if there's nothing on in the evening, I'll go home. More often than not, there's a dinner engagement. My wife comes to quite a lot of these, so at least we see each other.

J: When do you get to bed?

PJ: Rarely before midnight. I always read a book for half an hour before going to sleep.

J: Right, thank you, Mr Johnson …

Answers to the listening task

Events		Sequence
a.	Visit the plant	10
b.	Look at the post	6
c.	Have breakfast	3
d.	Meetings with Finance and Sales Directors	8
e.	Read a book	14
f.	Get up	1
g.	Dinner engagement	13
h.	Leave for the office	5
i.	Go for a jog	2
j.	Lunch in the canteen	9
k.	Management/Board meetings	11
l.	Read the newspapers	4
m.	Meeting with deputy	7
n.	Finish work	12
o.	Go to sleep	15

KEY – Unit 9

3. CONTROLLED PRACTICE

(Note: There are other appropriate answers.)

A.

A: *When do you get up?*
B: Usually at six. At least, my alarm clock goes off at six!
A: *Do you have breakfast straight away?*
B: No, I don't have breakfast straight away; first I go for a run.
A: *So, when do you sit down for/to have breakfast?*
B: I sit down for breakfast about seven.
A: *What do you do after breakfast?*
B: After breakfast I read the papers.
A: *Which papers do you read/take?*
B: Oh, The Guardian and The Independent.
A: *When do you leave for the office?*
B: I usually leave for the office about eight and I'm behind my desk by eight-thirty.
A: *What do you do first?*
B: I sort through the mail first.
A: *Do you have a secretary?*
B: No, I don't have a secretary. I wish I had!
A: *Do you always work in the office?*
B: No, I sometimes travel abroad.
A: *How often do you go/travel abroad?*
B: Oh, about four times a year. Usually to America.

B.

1. I *occasionally* travel abroad./*Occasionally* I travel abroad.
2. I *often* have meetings.
3. I *sometimes* see the Managing Director./*Sometimes* I see the Managing Director.
4. I *hardly ever* see the Chairman.
5. I *always* catch the seven o'clock bus.

KEY Unit 10

1. LISTENING

Tapescript

In this unit you will hear a business meeting. The managers at the meeting are discussing the current projects of various departments.

MD: OK, let's have a look very briefly at the current departmental projects. Why don't we start with EDP? What are you working on at the moment?

EDP: We're doing a user study for the installation of the new micros. So we're talking to all the new users at the moment.

MD: Right, what about Finance? I believe you

KEY – Unit 10

	are thinking of changing our accounting system.
FM:	Yes, that's right. We're having problems with the old system so we're looking into a new accounting system.
MD:	Fine, let's move on to Marketing. Are you working on any special projects?
MM:	Not really; but we are planning an advertising campaign for our new product.
MD:	Interesting. I look forward to seeing it. What about Production?
PM:	Well, as you know, we are currently installing the new automated assembly line.
MD:	Of course. You must be pretty busy. Personnel, what are you doing?
PeM:	We're trying to recruit new young graduates at the moment.
MD:	How's that going?
PeM:	Fine.
MD:	Well, the Administration Department are not represented here today. They are moving to new offices next week, so they've got their hands full. Research and Development are also very busy – they're testing the new prototype. That just leaves Transport and Management Services. John?
TM:	The Transport Department is rationalising the distribution network – so we're hoping for some big cost cuts in the near future.
MD:	Good. And Management Services?
MSM:	Well, we haven't got anything we're working on just at the moment but we are running a series of quality training seminars next month.
MD:	Right, that just about covers it.

Answers to the the listening task

Projects/fixed plans	Department
Plan advertising campaign	*Marketing*
Test new prototype	*Research and Development*
Move to new offices	*Administration*
Do user study	*EDP*
Rationalise distribution network	*Transport*
Run quality training seminars	*Management Services*
Look into new accounting system	*Finance*
Try to recruit new graduates	*Personnel*
Install automated assembly line	*Production*

3. CONTROLLED PRACTICE

A.

MD:	At the moment, the market *is expanding*. So this is an opportunity we must take. Our advertsing agency *is working on* a new campaign for next month. Now, what about Production?
PM:	Currently we *are running at* 75% capacity – so, that gives us some spare capacity.
MD:	Good, how *are* we *doing* on staffing levels in the factory?
PM:	We *are finding* it difficult to recruit technicians. There seems to be a shortage on the job market.
MD:	What *are* you *planning* to do about it?
PM:	Well, we *are thinking* of using a recruitment agency. A chap from a local agency *is*

KEY – Unit 10

MD: Fine, what about cash flow? The upturn in the market is going to be a drain on cash.

FM: That's right. At the moment, we *are managing* on an overdraft of about £50,000 and our current debts *are approaching* £85,000. I can go and talk to the Bank Manager about it. We've always been a good customer.

MD: Yes, do that as soon as possible. Finally, training. We're going to need some more sales reps and technicians in production. What *is happening* at the moment in training?

TM: We *are teaching* a refresher sales course but we've got spare capacity …

coming in to see me on Monday to talk about it.

B.

I'm *showing* Ms Patel around the plant.

I'm *giving* a demonstration of the new software to the Marketing Manager.

I'm *working on* the new promotion from about 10.00 on Tuesday morning, but what about early Tuesday morning?

I'm *having* a breakfast meeting with Mr Smith.

I'm *discussing* the new prototype from two till four. We're *having* drinks with Jan at five.

Sorry, I'm *picking up* Mr Steiner at the airport at three.

Are you *going* to the sales meeting on Wednesday morning?

KEY Unit 11

1. LISTENING   Tapescript

In this unit you will hear three telephone calls. In each call one of the speakers agrees to send a letter.

Call 1

A: I'm phoning about the letter I wrote to you.

B: Just a moment, I'll get it … the one dated 15 November?

A: That's right. I asked for a quotation for a consultancy contract in December.

B: Yes, I see. Haven't we replied to it?

A: No, and as I said in the letter, we need it urgently.

B: Right, I'm sorry. I don't know why this has happened. I'll get back to you this afternoon.

Call 2

A: I'm phoning about the job advertised in *The Times* for the post of Office Manager.

B: Yes, have you put your application in writing?

A: Yes, I sent in my application two weeks ago.

B: Fine, then you'll be hearing from us in the near future.

A: I realise that. I just wanted to let you know my availability.

B: Right, go ahead.

KEY – Unit 11

A: Well, I can start the job from the beginning of April.
B: Right, I'll make a note of that but can you put it in writing?
A: Yes, of course. I'll get a letter in the post today.

Call 3

A: You know that hotel you recommended in your last letter?
B: Yes, you mean the one in Southern Italy?
A: Right. Well I've lost the letter and I wanted to book in for a couple of weeks this summer.
B: Just a moment, I'll see if I can find the address … I'm sorry I can't find it.
A: Doesn't matter. Could you drop me a line?
B: Of course. I'll do that later this week.
A: Great. Nice talking to you. Bye.
B: Bye.

Answers to the listening task

Letter A: Telephone call 3
Letter B: Telephone call 1
Letter C: Telephone call 2

3. CONTROLLED PRACTICE

(Note: Other answers are possible.)

A.

Re: International Sales Workshop 5 November

Dear Ms Fisher

I am writing to inform you that, unfortunately, we have had to cancel our November workshop. However, we can include your staff in the October 8 workshop instead if this is convenient.

I regret that we were unable to inform you of this change earlier, and I hope you will be able to attend at this earlier date.

I would appreciate it if you could let me know *as soon as possible* the names of your staff who will be attending on October 8.

I am sure that your staff will find the workshop both useful and informative.

Yours *sincerely*

B.

Re: *International Sales Workshop 8 October*

Dear *Mr Reading*

This is to confirm that five members of our staff will be able to attend the October workshop.

Please find attached the names and addresses of the five participants. These are not the same five people as were to attend the November workshop.

I would be grateful if you could send me five copies of the workshop programme and maps showing the location of the Institute.

I look forward to meeting you on 8 October.

Yours *sincerely*

4. TRANSFER

(Note: Other answers are possible.)

Dear Mr Matthews

With reference to your letter of 25 May, I am pleased to *confirm my participation at this year's conference in July.*

I would be grateful *if you could send me further details about the programme.*

Unfortunately, *I will not be able to give an update on last year's talk. I am afraid that pressure of work will not allow time to prepare a talk.*

However, *I look forward to attending the conference again.*

KEY Unit 12

1. Listening   Tapescript

In this unit you will hear the Sales Director talking about the sales figures of three of her company's products.

Before I go on to talk about the sales targets for this year, let's have a look at the performance of our three main products over the last six years. Now, as you know, we launched three models the same year, in order to capture the full range of the market.

This graph, here, shows the progress of our top-of-the-range model – the A1456. As you can see, sales reached a peak just one year after launch. The following two years sales levelled off at around 400,000. Then sales decreased to a figure of 330,000 by the end of year five. Finally, last year sales fell to only 250,000 units.

OK, let's turn to the middle-of-the-range product, the B2456. As I said, this model was launched in the same year as the A1456, but sales progress has been somewhat different. In the first three years, sales rose steadily to a peak of 550,000 at the end of year three. The following year sales fell badly to 450,000. Then in year 5 they picked up again to settle around 500,000. They remained constant at this figure in year 6.

Finally, our cheapest model, the C3456. If we look at the figures for years 1 and 2, we see that sales increased rapidly in the second year to reach 250,000, then in the third year they rose again by 200,000 to reach 450,000. Fourth year sales were also good – the end-of-year figure went up to 580,000. Year 5 sales dropped slightly – they were down to 550,000 and this figure was maintained last year. I'm sure you'll agree, these results are excellent.

Answers to the listening task

Graph 1: C3456
Graph 2: B2456
Graph 3: A1456

3. Controlled practice

A1456
1. Sales *reached* a peak just one year after launch.
2. The following two years sales *levelled off* at 400,000.
3. Then sales *decreased* to a figure of 330,000 by the end of year five.
4. Last year sales *fell* to only 250,000 units.

B2456
5. In the first three years, sales *rose* steadily.
6. In the following year sales *fell* badly.
7. Then in year five they *picked up* again.
8. They *remained constant* at this figure in year six.

C3456
9. Sales *increased* rapidly in the second year to reach 250,000.
10. In year three they *reached* 450,000.
11. Year four figures *went up* to 580,000.
12. In year five sales *dropped* slightly.

KEY – Unit 12

4. TRANSFER   Pair work

Student B:

1. Listen to Student A's description of the performance of a product (sales and prices). As you listen, complete the graph below.

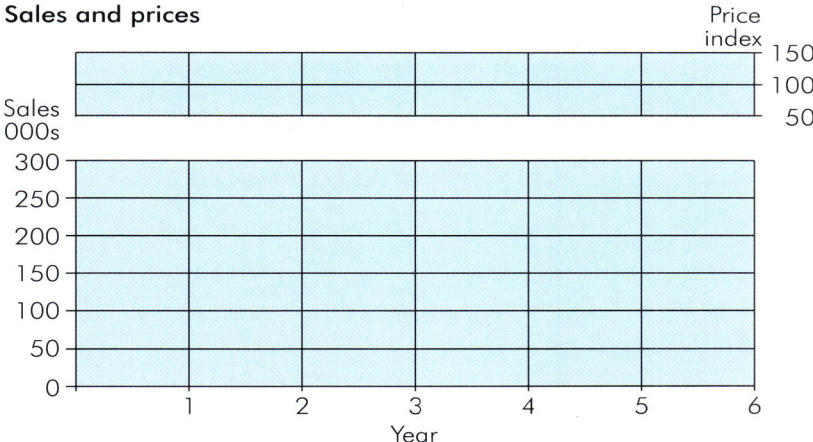

2. The graph below shows the performance of a product (turnover and profits). Describe it to Student A.

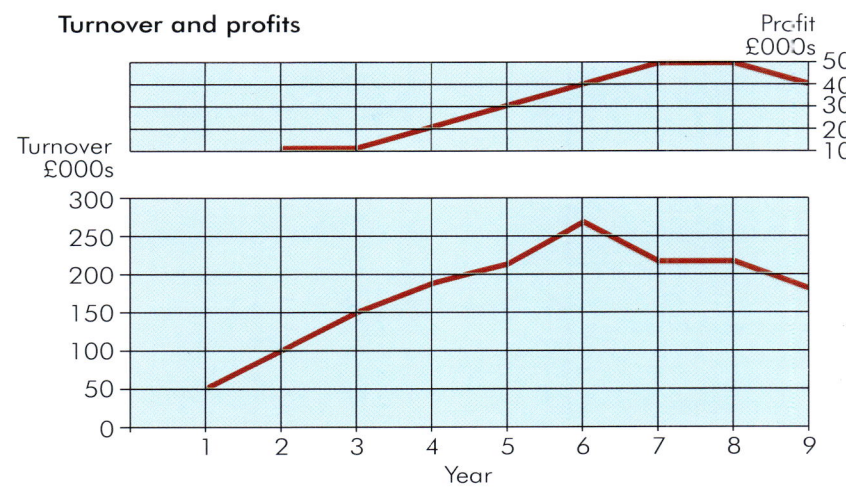

— 123 —

KEY Unit 13

1. LISTENING — Tapescript

In this unit you will hear the Sales Director talking about the company's sales figures for the future.

Right, let's move on to targets for next year and our plans over the next five years.

As you saw earlier, sales for the A1456 have been falling for some time and last year were only 250,000. We expect sales will be roughly the same next year, although we will be starting a large-scale promotion in March. If this is successful, perhaps we can boost sales to 300,000. Still, I prefer to keep our forecast figure at 250,000.

Now, we come to the B2456. We don't expect sales will be quite as high as last year as we are not going to push this product this year. My view is that sales should reach 450,000. This may be a little optimistic for a product which is now six years old, but I think we should be able to achieve it.

We are sure the sales of C3456 will start to recover. Indeed, sales may go as high as 650,000 next year. However, I have set the target slightly lower, at 600,000.

Now, let's look at our medium-term plans. Next year we intend to launch our new product – the D4456 – and we are sure sales will take off very quickly. We estimate first year sales figures at 200,000 and we hope that within three years the D4456 will replace the A1456. We intend to stop production on the A1456 within five years.

Finally, R and D are working on a new medium-range product and they hope to have this ready in two years' time, so we could be launching it within three or four years.

Answers to the listening task

Graph 1: B2456
Graph 2: D4456
Graph 3: A1456
Graph 4: C3456

3. CONTROLLED PRACTICE

(Note: Other answers are possible.)

2. Sales of A1456 may/could be above target.
3. The D4456 is going to be launched next year.
4. C3456 sales will/are going to reach their target.
5. We expect the D4456 will replace the A1456.
6. The new medium-range product could be ready in two years' time.
7. A large-scale promotion is going to be carried out by the sales team.
8. We hope total sales will be around £1,250,000 next year.
9. The campaign should/will probably be successful.
10. The product may/could be ready in five years' time.

4. TRANSFER — Pair work

Student B:
1. You are a supplier of office equipment. A customer (Student A) will telephone you about delivery dates. Use the information overleaf to answer his/her questions. Use the language from

KEY – Unit 13

the Presentation section to indicate the degree of likelihood.

Product	Delivery date	Likelihood
office desks	10 June	probability
office chairs	30 May	certainty
calendars	1 July	possibility
year planners	30 October	probability
filing cabinets	7 August	certainty
security cupboards	1 September	possibility

When you have finished, compare your table with Student A's notes.

2. You are a customer. Phone your supplier (Student A) and find out about the delivery dates of the following products. Note the degree of likelihood of the supplier keeping to these dates.

Product	Delivery date	Likelihood
adjustable keyboard		
mouse		
colour scanner		
colour printer		
floppy discs		
21-inch colour screen		

Ask questions like:
When can we expect delivery?
When do you think …?

When you have finished, compare your notes with Student A's information.

KEY Unit 14

1. LISTENING — Tapescript

In this unit you will hear an end-of-year presentation by a company chairman.

I'd like to spend a few minutes of your time looking back over the year. I'm going to divide my review into three areas: firstly, financial, secondly, personnel and finally technology.

On the financial front, the results have been very pleasing. Turnover has increased by 14%, costs have dropped by 3% and profits are up by 16%. So the company as a whole has performed well. Some business areas have done better than others. Export sales have done very well – especially in America, our largest export market. The domestic consumer market has been very competitive and will continue to be so – our results in this market have been rather disappointing – just 1% up compared with last year.

Right, let's move on to personnel. Our policy of personnel development through training and promotion opportunities has continued to be a great success. We have actually recruited 72 new staff, while 20 have retired – so there's a net balance of 52. The training department has expanded considerably and moved into new areas such as quality assurance and sales training.

Finally, technology. I thought you would be interested to have an update since this is vital for our future growth. Over the last year, our Research Department has thoroughly tested a new prototype engine. Results so far have looked promising. We have also invested heavily in a European technology programme which links industry with the universities.

Right, those are the three main areas – finance, personnel and technology. Are there any questions, before I go on? …

Answers to the listening task

End of year review
3 areas
1. Financial   a. Results   • turnover + 14%
                            • costs   – 3%
                            • profits   + 16%

              b. Exports – good esp America
              Domestic market - very competitive, only + 1%

2. Personnel a. Personnel development continued
              b. 72 recruited
                 20 retired
                 52 net increase
              c. training has expanded
                 new areas: quality assurance and sales

3. Technology a. Research Dept has tested prototype engine
              b. Have invested in European technology programme

KEY – Unit 14

3. CONTROLLED PRACTICE

A.

1. Turnover *increased* by 14% last year.
2. The company *has had* disappointing results recently.
3. The domestic consumer market *has been* very competitive.
4. Two years ago we *launched* an updated product.
5. We *have recruited* 20 junior managers.
6. *Have* you ever *visited* Australia?
7. We *went* there last June.
8. We *have* not *received* the results of the tests yet.
9. *Did* you *see* the report?
   Yes, it was interesting.
10. Three senior managers *have retired* this year.

B.

Irregular verbs

Present simple/ infinitive	Past simple	Past participle
do	did	done
drive	drove	driven
eat	ate	eaten
fly	flew	flown
go	went	gone
have	had	had
make	made	made
send	sent	sent
sleep	slept	slept
speak	spoke	spoken
write	wrote	written

KEY – Unit 14

4. TRANSFER — Pair work

Student B:

1. Student A is going to ask you a number of questions. Your answers should be in either the present perfect or past simple.

2. Find out whether Student A has or hasn't done the things on the list opposite. If the answer is yes, ask for further information about when/where/why he/she did them.

All introductory questions should be in the present perfect. All questions for further information should be in the past simple.

e.g. Have you (ever) travelled by hovercraft?
Where did you go to?
When was that?
Why did you go there?

1. Go to a conference
2. Send a fax to Britain
3. Travel first class on a plane
4. Miss an important meeting
5. Eat Chinese food
6. Write a letter in English
7. Go to a health club
8. Have a holiday abroad

KEY Unit 15

1. LISTENING — Tapescript

In this unit you will hear a business meeting. The three participants in the meeting are discussing company strategy.

A: We need to define a new strategy but this strategy must be flexible enough to take account of changing market conditions.

B: I agree. Our main objective must be to gain market share, and to do this we must reduce prices.

A: So are you sure that if we reduce prices, our market share will increase?

B: Yes, I'm sure.

C: That's probably true, but if we reduce prices, our margins will be lower and that will cut profits.

B: In the short term that's right, but we can slowly increase production, and with increased production, we'll cut unit costs.

C: That's really a long-term prospect. Unit costs can only come down if we invest in new plant and machinery.

A: Let's stop there a minute and try to define our strategy in two directions – firstly, the market and secondly, manufacturing. Do we agree that increased market share is the objective?

C: No, I don't agree. I think we should go for higher profitability. If we can upgrade the product, we'll get better prices and therefore higher profits.

B: Look, the market is already very competitive and getting more so. If we increase prices, whatever the quality, sales will drop rapidly.

KEY – Unit 15

A: Right, let's look at it from the other point of view – manufacturing.

C: Well, if we can reduce costs in manufacturing, that must put us in a strong position to adapt to the market. The only way we can be flexible enough is to sub-contract more of the production.

B: But it'll mean job losses if we do that.

C: Yes, but the jobs that remain will be more secure.

Answers to the listening task

1. d   5. g
2. e   6. c
3. a   7. h
4. f   8. b

3. CONTROLLED PRACTICE

(Note: There are other possible answers.)

1. Our customers will be more satisfied / We will have more satisfied customers } if we improve the delivery service.

2. If we rationalise production, unit costs will be reduced.

3. There will be job losses / We will have job losses } if we rationalise production.

4. If we install robots, { our labour costs will be lower. / we will lower our labour costs.

5. There will be a price war / We will have a price war } if competitors enter the market.

6. We can/will charge higher prices if we upgrade the product.

7. We can/will earn larger profits if we increase our margins.

8. If we do no research there will be no new products.
   If we don't do any research there won't be any new products.

9. If we don't offer better salaries, we won't attract the best people.

10. If there are fewer meetings / If we have fewer meetings } we will have more time to do the job.

4. TRANSFER   Pair work

Student B:
1. Answer Student A's questions like this:
   If my company moves to another location, I will …
2. Then think up some 'If' questions to ask Student A.

KEY Unit 16

1. LISTENING   Tapescript

In this unit a Sales Manager talks about his company and its main competitors.

Let's look at the competition. Now, our main competitor – Benton – entered the market in 1982 – ten years later than us. But since then they have grown more rapidly and are now the biggest in terms of market share. Why? Mainly because of their product development. Their products are better, sold at lower prices and presented more attractively. At the moment their main weakness is that they have the lowest profitability.

Now, our second major competitor is Zecron. They entered the market at the same time as us. They have a lower market share than us and their products are sold at slightly higher prices. However, their annual return shows greater profitability and much heavier investment in plant and machinery over the last two years. So they are in a good position to overtake us soon.

The last competitor is Mansell. They have been in the market slightly longer than us and Zecron. They have a much smaller market share, but their products are sold at the top end of the market at much higher prices. As a result they achieve the best profitability of the four companies with much lower turnover.

So, what can we say about our own position? Well, our products are medium-price but less attractive than Benton's. We're getting a problem with reliability. Certainly Benton's range has a reputation for being much more reliable. Our market share is higher than Zecron and Mansell, but they are more profitable than us. So, we must become more competitive during the next two years if we are to hold on to our market share and increase profitability.

Answers to the listening task

	Age in market (1 = oldest)	Market share (1 = biggest)	Product price (1 = cheapest)	Profitability (1 = most profitable)
Brotherton	2	2	2	3
Benton	4	1	1	4
Zecron	2	3	3	2
Mansell	1	4	4	1

3. CONTROLLED PRACTICE

1. Mansell have been in the market *the longest*.
2. Brotherton entered the market *earlier* than Benton.
3. Benton entered the market ten years *later* than Brotherton.
4. Benton have *the largest/biggest* market share.
5. Mansell have a much *smaller/lower* market share than Brotherton.
6. Benton's products are sold at *the lowest* prices.

KEY – Unit 16

7. Mansell's products are sold at *much higher* prices than Brotherton's.
8. Zecron's products are *slightly more expensive* than Brotherton's.
9. Mansell is *the most* profitable company.
10. Brotherton is *more profitable* than Benton.

4. TRANSFER   Pair work

Student B:
1. Use the table below to answer Student A's questions.
Answer like this:

R and D Building Society is the most *profitable*.

Cittabank is more *profitable* than *Elton Bank*.

Company	Turnover (1 = biggest)	Profitability (1 = most profitable)	Share capital (1 = largest)	Employees (1 = most)
Cittabank	1	2	1	4
R and D Building Society	2	1	3	1
Elton Bank	4	3	2	3
Finance Banking	3	4	4	2

2. Ask Student A questions so that you can complete the table below by inserting ranking figures (1–4). Ask questions like:

Which is the most _____ company?

Is _____ more _____ than _____ ?

Company	Age in market (1 = oldest)	Technology (1 = most modern)	Premises (1 = largest)	Employees (1 = best trained)
A G Oil				
Natelcom				
RAM				
Chand Chemicals				

KEY Unit 17

1. Listening — Tapescript

In this unit you will hear a telephone conversation about the timing of a construction project.

A: I'm phoning about the timing for the Vienna project.

B: Right, we've got a starting date for that, haven't we?

A: Yes, we begin a pilot study on 5 November.

B: Right, how long is that expected to last?

A: We should finish the study in three weeks.

B: Good, then what's the next stage?

A: Well, we've got a meeting with the contractor scheduled for 1 December. If everything goes according to plan, we'll sign the contract then. And work can commence at the beginning of January.

B: So what's the first stage?

A: Well, excavation will begin in January and is due to finish by the middle of February. Now, after that we could have a problem.

B: What's that?

A: You remember we've sub-contracted the German firm to do the foundations. They promised to start in the middle of February. They are now saying they can't.

B: Right, I'll get on to them. When are they due to finish the foundations?

A: In the contract, it says by 28 February.

B: I see, and then?

A: Construction work should begin on 5 March. We're on a pretty tight schedule. All the work has to be done in March and April.

B: OK. I see the problem. I'll phone you back in the afternoon at about three. Bye.

A: Goodbye.

Answers to the listening task

1. Pilot study
2. Meeting with contractor
3. Excavation
4. Foundations
5. Construction

3. Controlled practice

1. The work is due to begin *at/by* the end of April.
2. We are hoping to meet the engineer *at* the weekend.
3. We expect to sign the contract sometime *in* June.
4. We arrived *in* time to see them leave.
5. They are scheduled to finish *by/in* the middle of July.
6. I arranged to meet him *at* 15.30 *on* Tuesday.
7. The plane took off precisely *on* time.
8. We are busiest *in* spring.
9. The contract must be finalised *by* the end of the month, at the latest.
10. He phoned me *at* one o'clock *at* night.

KEY – Unit 17

4. TRANSFER   Pair work

Student B:
1. Use the project planner to answer Student A's questions.

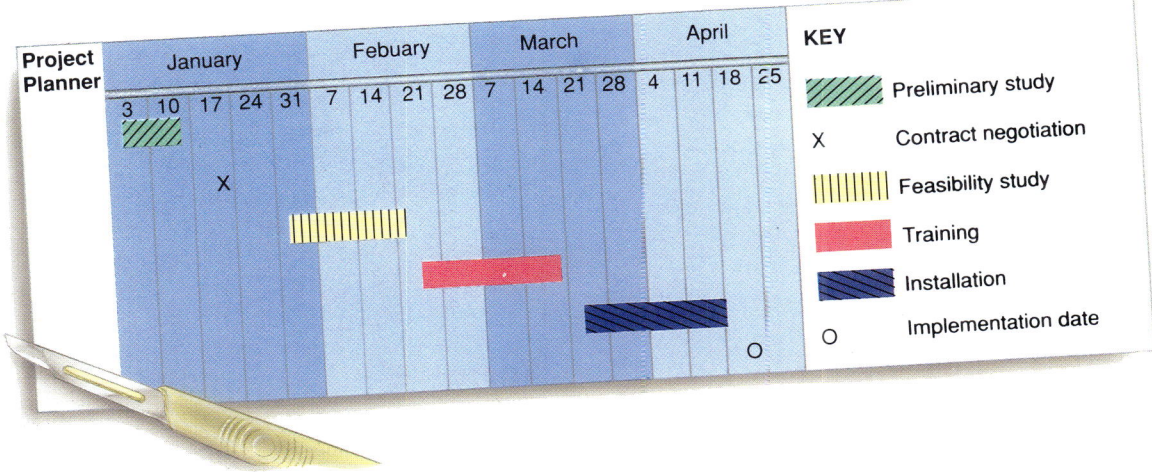

2. Student A will describe a recent event. Listen and take notes about the sequence and timing of events.

KEY Unit 18

1. LISTENING   Tapescript

In this unit a Plant Manager shows some visitors around an assembly plant producing printed circuit boards, and takes them to the three main parts of the plant.

Right. Basically there are three parts of the plant – the supply area, the assembly area and the despatch area.

So let's start here in the supply area. The raw materials come by truck and are off-loaded onto a conveyor. The conveyor takes them into the supply room. As you can see, this room is divided into three storage areas. On the shelves we store the electronic components. Stacked up against the wall are the boards and between the boards and the shelves we store the chemicals used in the process.

KEY – Unit 18

Right, let's go through into the assembly area. In this first part, the boards are cut into shape. There is one passing through the cutter now and then holes are drilled into the board … the boards come out of the drilling machine and then the components are inserted into the holes. If we go across to the other side, you'll see the boards coming off a conveyor.

So the assembled boards then go into the despatch area, which is behind this door. The boards are sorted according to their type and size over here – on this big table. Then they are stacked in front of this table here. And finally they are packed in boxes ready for despatch.

Answers to the listening task

1. c	6. h	11. m
2. a	7. j	12. o
3. e	8. f	13. l
4. b	9. g	14. k
5. d	10. i	15. n

3. CONTROLLED PRACTICE

1. London lies *on* the River Thames.
2. I'll meet you *in* the airport.
3. I'll meet you *at* the airport.
4. I can't find Tweedale Street at all. It must be *off* the map.
5. Cologne is *between* Bonn and Düsseldorf.
6. We walked *through* the main hall to the conference room.
7. My car is parked *in front of* the building.
8. Where's Peter? He just walked *out of* the office.
9. Come *into* my office. We can talk in private there.
10. On a clear day, you can see *across* the Channel *to* France.
11. Now I remember the bridge. It's *over* the River Avon.
12. Exhausted after the meeting, he dropped his briefcase *onto* the desk.
13. He put the document *in/into* the safe.
14. I took the letter *out of* the filing cabinet.
15. The ship sails *from* Hamburg *to* Stockholm.
16. The tunnel will be built 100 metres *below* sea level.

4. TRANSFER   Pair work

Student B:
1. Tell Student A where the furniture shown on your plan is located.

2. Now complete the office plan to show where the following items of furniture are. Student A will tell you where they should be.

telephone   easy chairs   coat stand
meetings table   drinks cabinet

3. When you have finished, compare your plan with Student A's. They should look the same.

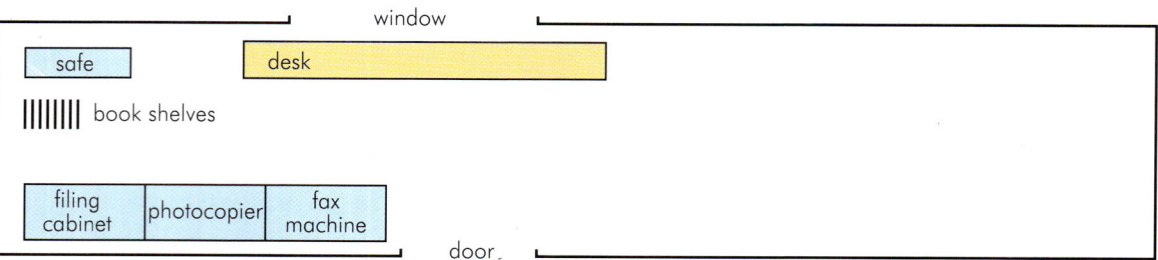

KEY Unit 19

1. LISTENING   Tapescript

In this unit you will hear a conversation between a market researcher and a consumer.

A: Right. I'd just like to check some details first. It's Mr and Mrs J. Reynolds, isn't it?
B: Yes.
A: The address is 21 Pine Avenue?
B: Yes.
A: Your telephone number is 56822, is that right?
B: No, it's 56882.
A: Thanks. Now I hope you don't mind if I ask you some personal questions?
B: No, go ahead.
A: First, do you own this house?
B: Yes, we do.
A: How many people live in it?
B: Well there's myself, my husband and two sons.
A: So four of you. Where does your husband work?
B: He works at Courtaulds.
A: And do you work outside of the home?
B: No, I'm a freelance book designer. I work at home.
A: Right, your sons are at school then?
B: Yes, that's right.
A: Do they go to the local school?
B: No, they both go into town to the Independent Boys' School.
A: Now, both you and your husband have a car?
B: Yes, we do.
A: Roughly how many miles do you do a year?
B: Well, about 5,000.
A: Your husband's car is on the firm, is that right?
B: Yes.
A: How many holidays a year do you take?
B: Normally two.
A: In this country or abroad?
B: Usually a summer holiday abroad and a week somewhere in Britain in the autumn.
A: Somewhere by the sea?
B: No, we normally go to Scotland walking.
A: Right, just a couple more questions; then I'm finished. Do you mind telling me how much you normally spend on your summer holiday?
B: Well, I suppose about £2,000.
A: And this year you plan to go abroad?
B Yes, Greece actually.
A: Well, thank you very much, Mrs Reynolds. You've been very helpful.
B: You're welcome.

Answers to the listening task

Name   *J Reynolds*
Address   *21 Pine Avenue*
Telephone   *56882*
Accommodation
Own home ✔   Rent ☐   Hotel ☐   Other ☐
Number in home *4*

— 135 —

KEY – Unit 19

Place of work: Husband   *Courtaulds*
                 Wife   *at home*

Place of study: Child 1   *Independent Boys'
                            School*
                 Child 2   *Independent Boys'
                            School*

Holidays per year *2*

Location   *summer — abroad*
             autumn — Scotland

Money spent on next summer holiday *£2,000*

Location of next holiday *Greece*

3. CONTROLLED PRACTICE

1. Your name is P. Thomson, isn't it?
2. Your address is 45 Main Street (isn't it/is that right)?
3. And you own your own house (don't you/is that right)?
4. Where do you work?
5. Have you worked there for long?
6. How do you travel/get to work?
7. Do you have any children?
8. How old are they?
9. Are they at school?
10. What do they do in the evenings?
11. How often do you go to the cinema?
12. Do you ever go to restaurants?
13. When do you go to bed?

KEY Unit 20

1. LISTENING   Tapescript

In this unit you will hear a business meeting. The participants at the meeting are discussing the budgets for four company departments.

P: Right, let's get started. Now, you've all seen the budget proposals for next year. Have you got anything to say?

J: I think the research figure is too low. We should increase it by at least 5%.

P: Well, we could do that, but it means less money for the other departments. I think it should stay the same.

S: I agree with John. We could reduce the figure for marketing — that would allow us to increase the budget for research.

P: I felt marketing needed a good figure this year. They've got a big launch mid-year. I think they couldn't manage with less.

J: I'm sure they could and …

P: Just a moment. Let's look at the other two department budgets. That's production and sales.

J: Well, we can't cut the production budget, that's for sure. I don't know about sales.

KEY – Unit 20

S: Why do you say we can't cut production's budget? They had a big investment last year. Well, surely they could manage on less this year?

P: Yes, I think I agree. Production ought to manage with less this year, having spent so much last year.

S: A small cut in the production budget might mean we could increase the research figure.

P: Right, I'll put that to the Production Manager. Finally, what about sales?

S: I think it's a bit high. They might save a bit by spending less on the after-sales side.

P: John, any views?

J: Well, I think we should spend more on sales.

P: That's out of the question. The figure shouldn't be changed.

Answers to the listening task
Budget proposals

Department	Budget	Peter	John	Susan
Research	£25,000	OK	+	+
Marketing	£45,000	OK	–	–
Production	£145,000	–	OK	–
Sales	£55,000	OK	+	–

3. CONTROLLED PRACTICE

1. We should/ought to reduce the sales budget.
2. Marketing might accept a cut in their budget.
3. We can't cut the production budget.
4. We could spend more on direct sales activities.
5. We should/ought to reduce the total budget.
6. Research can't continue on this budget.
7. More money could be made available.
8. We shouldn't/ought not to cut the marketing budget.
9. Sales might not reach their target.
10. Production could need more money later in the year.

Glossary

Key: adj = adjective;   adv = adverb;   n = noun;   v = verb;   inf = informal;   pl = plural

A

abroad (adv) to/in another country: *The sales director is abroad on business.*
absence (n) time/period away from work
  absent (adj) not present, not at work: *Please let your section head know if you will be absent for a longer period.*
  absenteeism (n) regular absence from work: *If motivation decreases, absenteeism is likely to increase.*
absorb (v) integrate a smaller item into a larger whole: *Head Office has absorbed the losses of our French subsidiary.*
access 1. (n) entry to something: *We have access to classified information.*
2. (v) gain entry into computer data files: *They shouldn't be able to access this file.*
account (n) record of financial transactions
  accountable (adj) responsible
  accountancy (n) work of an accountant
  accountant (n) person qualified to keep a company's accounts
  accounting (n) job of recording money paid and received by a company
  accounts (n pl) financial records of a business: *The bank would like to see the accounts.*
achieve (v) succeed in doing something
  achievement (n) the successful completion of something, something successfully completed
acknowledge (v) confirm that something has arrived: *We acknowledge receipt of the goods.*
acquire (v) buy, obtain: *We acquired a company.*
  acquisition (n) gaining/getting, e.g. of a company, shares, etc.
activity (n) type of business: *Our main activity is export/import trade.*
actual (adj) real: *Our actual results were better than forecast.*

adapt (v) change
adjust (v) change/modify something: *We must adjust the price to reflect inflation.*
administration (n) organisation and control of a company
  administer (v) organise, control
adopt (v) choose, decide on: *We adopted a new strategy.*
advertise (v) announce something is for sale
  ad (n inf) short for advertisement
  advertisement (n) notice/announcement that something is for sale
  advertising (n) the business of designing ads: *She's in advertising.*
advice (n) recommendation(s) about what you should do: *His advice was to close the factory.*
  advise (v) recommend what should be done
agenda (n) order of topics to be discussed at a meeting: *The first topic on the agenda is salaries.*
agent (n) person who represents a company
allocate (v) give money or other resources in certain proportions: *In the budget we allocated most of the money to marketing.*
analyse (v) study in detail: *We analysed the accounts.*
  analysis (n) detailed study, investigation
  analyst (n) person who analyses
annual (adj) yearly: *the annual accounts*
  annual general meeting (n) (AGM) a meeting of all the shareholders in a company
apply (v) ask for something (in writing): *We applied for a loan.*
  application (n) act of applying: *We filled in an application form.*
appoint (v) choose someone for a job: *We have decided to appoint a new sales manager.*
  appointment (n) 1. choice of someone for a new job

Glossary

2. arrangement for a meeting: *We fixed an appointment for four o'clock.*
appreciate (v) 1. be thankful for: *I appreciated your help.* 2. understand: *I appreciate your problems.* 3. increase in value: *My shares have appreciated by 10%.*
approve (v) agree to pass officially: *The Board approved the new plan.*
area (n) region: *His sales area is the North East.*
assemble (v) put (a product) together from component parts
   assembly (n) putting (a product) together: *We have automated the assembly line.*
   assembly line (n) production system where the product moves slowly through the factory with new parts added as it goes along
assess (v) estimate the value of: *The property was assessed at £20,000.*
   assessment (n) calculation of value: *a tax assessment*
asset (n) something of value which is owned by a company: *The company's major asset is its property.*
assist (v) help
audit (n) examination of the accounts of a company
automate (v) make something work automatically, i.e. without the work of people
average 1. (n) the number which is calculated by adding several figures together and then dividing by the number of figures: *The sales average has been around 250 units.* 2. (adj) middle: *the average price*

B

back 1. (n) opposite of front: *Please sign the cheque on the back.* 2. (adj) from the past: *We have a lot of back orders.* 3. (v) support: *The bank backed my new venture.*
bad debt (n) debt which will not be paid
balance (n) amount which makes the total credits and debits equal
   balance sheet (n) statement of the financial position of a company or business at a certain moment

bank statement (n) written statement showing transactions and balance of an account
bankrupt (adj) unable to pay debts and put in the hands of a receiver: *He was declared bankrupt. He went bankrupt.*
   bankruptcy (n) state of being bankrupt
bargain 1. (v) discuss in order to reach agreement on price/conditions 2. (n) item at a good (cheap) price
base (n) place where a company has its headquarters
   based (adj) located
basic (adj) minimum that can be expected; what everything else depends on: *Older workers will, of course, still be interested in basic pay.*
beat (v) win over (someone) in a fight: *We have beaten our competitors to be first on the market.*
behave (v) act
   behaviour (n) way of acting
benefit 1. (v) profit 2. (n) 1. advantage, profit: *Many company benefits are provided simply because it's the accepted practice.* 2. money provided as a right under a state or private insurance scheme
   fringe benefits (n pl) extra benefits such as a car, private health insurance provided by a company
bid (n & v) offer to buy something at a certain price
   takeover bid (n) bid to buy a company
bill 1. (n) written list of money to be paid: *This bill does not include VAT.* 2. (v) send a bill to someone
black (adj) not allowed by law: *black market*
   in the black in credit
blue chips (n pl) shares with the highest status as investments, usually shares of well-established companies
blue-collar (adj) relating to manual work: *Your local newspaper is usually the best source of blue-collar jobs.*
board of directors (n) group of people chosen by the shareholders to develop company policy
bonus (n) additional payment
books (n pl) the financial records of a company
   bookkeeper (n) person who keeps the financial records of a company
boom (n) time when business activity is

Glossary

increasing: *We must take advantage of the economic boom.*
boost (v) increase
borrow (v) accept money from someone on the basis that you will repay it later
bottom 1. (adj) lowest: *rock-bottom price*
2. (v) bottom out, reach the lowest point
branch (n) local office of a large business: *We have branches throughout the country.*
brand (n) product which can be recognised by a name
break even (v) balance costs and revenue, not make a profit or a loss: *We just broke even last year.*
    breakeven point point at which revenue equals costs
bring forward (v) make earlier: *We brought the launch date forward to June 1st.*
brochure (n) publicity booklet giving information about a product/service: *They asked for a brochure about our services.*
budget (n) plan of forecast income and expenditure
bulk 1. (n) large quantity (of goods)
2. (adj) *We can offer you a discount for bulk purchase.*
bust (adj inf) bankrupt: *The firm went bust.*

call 1. (n) visit, telephone call: *The salesman plans to make seven calls.*
2. (v) telephone
    call on (v) visit
campaign (n) plan of action: *advertising campaign*
candidate (n) person who puts himself/ herself forward for a job: *Several managers normally interview one candidate*
canteen (n) factory restaurant
capacity (n) amount which can be produced: *We are working at full capacity.*
capital (n) money, property and assets used in a business
capture (v) take: *We captured 20% of the market.*
career (n) job or profession for which one is trained and which one intends to do throughout one's life: *People have to decide how important work and career are to be in their life.*
cash 1. (n) money in notes and coins
2. (v) exchange a cheque for cash
    cash flow (n) money coming into a company in sales less the money going out on purchases and overheads
catalogue [US **catalog**] (n) a sales publication which lists products and prices
CEO (n) US Chief Executive Officer
chain (n) number of shops belonging to one company
channel (n) means by which goods pass from one place to another: *The main distribution channel is through supermarkets.*
charge (n) payment to be made for a service: *There is no service charge included in the bill – it is at your discretion!*
chart (n) diagram which displays information visually
cheque (n) [US **check**] note ordering a bank to pay money to the person/company whose name is written on the cheque
chief (adj) most important: *This is the chief problem.*
claim 1. (n) request for money: *We put in an insurance claim after the accident.*
2. (v) ask for money: *We claimed $50,000 in damages.*
client (n) person or company buying a service
Co (n) abbreviation for company
commission (n) proportionate amount of money paid to a sales person/agent, usually a percentage of the sales made: *We offered the agent a 10% commission.*
commodity (n) goods sold in very large quantities, such as metals, foodstuffs
company (n) registered business
    limited (liability) company (ltd.) a private company where the shareholders are responsible for repaying debts to the value of their shares
    public limited company (plc) company whose shares can be bought on the Stock Exchange
compensate (v) give something such as money to someone for loss or damage
    compensation (n) something, usually money, given to someone for loss or damage

Glossary

compete (v) succeed in doing better than (another person/company): *It's difficult to compete with low-priced imports.*
    competition (n) process of trying to do better: *The competition is very fierce.*
    competitor (n) person/company that competes
    competitive (adj) of a product which competes well: *It's important to keep a competitive edge.*
competence (n) ability to do a job well, skill or efficiency: *If an organisation recruits from inside, employees see that competence is rewarded.*
component (n) part which will be put into a final product
condition (n) 1. general state 2. term of a contract
conflict (n) disagreement
consolidate (v) put the accounts of subsidiary companies into the parent company's accounts
constant (adj) fixed
consumer (n) person who buys goods or services
contract (n) legal agreement between two parties
contribute (v) give support (often money): *We contributed to the fund.*
    contribution (n) amount of support or money given
conveyor (n) moving belt for transport of products
core time (n) period of working day when all employees must be at work (see also **flexitime**): *However, you must all be here for core time from 10 till 3.*
corporate (adj) referring to the whole company: *Corporate advertising sells the company, not its products.*
cost (n) amount of money which has to be paid
    fixed costs costs which do not increase when production increases or decreases
    running costs costs of day-to-day management of a company
    cost-effective (adj) which gives value: *The scheme is cost-effective.*
credit (n & adj) time given to a customer to pay: *We normally give 3 months' credit.*
    letter of credit note from a bank allowing credit and promising to repay at a later date
    credit limit maximum amount that a customer can owe
    creditor (n) person who is owed money

crisis (n) dangerous/difficult/serious situation: *a banking crisis*
currency (n) money which is used in a particular country
current (adj) referring to the present time
    current account bank account from which a customer can withdraw money at any time
customer (n) person/company who buys goods
    customise (v) adapt a product for a particular customer
cut (n) decrease
cut-throat (adj) fierce, intense: *cut-throat competition*
cv (n) (= curriculum vitae) written statement of education and previous employment: *If you want to apply for the job, don't forget to send in a detailed CV.*

D

damages (n pl) money claimed for harm done: *We are claiming damages for unfair dismissal.*
deadline (n) date/time by which something has to be done: *The deadline is tomorrow morning.*
deal 1. (n) 1. business agreement: *We set up a deal with our agents.* 2. amount: *a great deal of money*. 2. (v) trade, buy and sell: *He deals in gold.*
    dealer (n) person who buys and sells: *a foreign exchange dealer*
debit 1. (n) money which is owed: *The debit column is the left-hand column in accounts.* 2. (v) debit an account: *to charge an account with a cost*
debt (n) money owed
    to get into debt
    to pay off a debt
    debtor (n) person who owes money
declare (v) make an official statement: *The company declared interim profits of $20 million.*
decline 1. (n) slow fall
2. (v) fall slowly
decrease (v) fall
deduct (v) subtract from the total figure: *After deducting all the costs, we actually made a loss.*
    deduction (n) subtraction from the total figure: *after deduction of tax*

Glossary

defect (n) fault, something wrong in the design of a machine
   defective (adj) not working properly
deficit (n) amount by which expenditure is higher than income: *The accounts show a deficit.*
deliver (v) transport goods to a customer
   delivery (n) transportation of goods to a customer
demand (n) 1. request for payment: *First demands were issued to all late payers.* 2. need for products and services at a certain price: *We are having difficulty meeting demand.*
department (n) part of an organisation: *The employment manager would like to talk to some of the company's supervisors and department heads.*
deposit (n) 1. money placed in a bank account 2. money paid in advance in order to reserve a product
depreciate (v) reduce the value of assets in the accounts over a certain time: *We depreciate business equipment over 5 years.*
   depreciation (n) reduction in the value of an asset
deputy (n) person who takes the place of another
despatch see: **dispatch**
dimensions (n pl) size
direct (v) manage, be in charge of: *He directs our sales operation.*
   direct mail (n) selling a product by sending information through the post
   director (n) person appointed by shareholders to help manage a company
   managing director UK [US **Chief Executive Officer**]
directory (n) reference book containing listings: *a telephone directory, a trade directory*
discount 1. (n) percentage reduction in a full price 2. (v) reduce the full price
dismiss (v) remove from employment, sack (inf)
dispatch 1. (n) sending goods to a customer: *dispatch department* 2. (v) send goods to customers
display 1. (n) show/exhibition of goods: *There was a display of the latest research at the trade fair in Frankfurt.* 2. (v) show, exhibit

distribute (v) send out goods from the manufacturer to the end user
   distribution (n) act of sending goods to end users
   distributor (n) person or company which sells goods for a manufacturer: *We are the sole distributors.*
diversify (v) extend into new business areas: *Although we are a chemicals company, we diversified into publishing.*
division (n) main part of a large organisation: *The job description indicates where the job is to be carried out in terms of location, plant, division, department, section.*
domestic (adj) referring to the home market
drop (v) fall
due (adj) owed: *This debt became due last week.*

E

earn (v) receive money for work
   earnings (n pl) salaries, profits, dividends, interest received
economic (adj) 1. providing enough money: *This project doesn't make economic sense.* 2. referring to state of the national economy: *There is an economic crisis.*
   economical (adj) money-saving: *an economical car*
   economist (n) person who specialises in the study of economics
   economy (n) financial organisation of a country: *a free market economy*
employ (v) take on or use a person as a paid worker: *During the year we employed an average of 65.*
   employee (n) person taken on as a paid worker
   employer (n) person or organisation that takes on paid workers
   employment (n) work, job(s)
enquire (v) ask
enter (v) go into: *We entered the market in 1980.*
entrepreneur (n) person who starts and runs a company/business
environment (n) surroundings: *To be classed as a*

Glossary

work accident, the accident must take place in the work environment.
evaluate (v) calculate the value of something: *The training and development manager plans, organises and evaluates training programmes.*
exhibit 1. (n) goods or services displayed at a fair or trade show
2. (v) display products or services at a show
    exhibition (n) show of goods
expand (v) get bigger: *The market is expanding.*
    expansion (n) increase in size
expenditure (n) amount of money spent: *Capital expenditure is the money we have spent on fixed assets.*
    expense (n) money spent: *We renovated the building at great expense.*
    expenses (n pl) money paid for covering extra costs: *The fee did not include travel expenses.*
expertise (n) particular knowledge or skill: *He has special expertise in computer systems.*

F

factor (n) thing which is important: *Price is an important factor when deciding our strategy.*
fee (n) money paid for service provided by a professional person such as a lawyer or a doctor
feedback (n) information about the results of an activity, given to a person so that changes can be made: *After the session we will give you feedback on your performance so that it can be improved.*
file 1. (n) a collection of documents on a subject: *According to my files we haven't prepared the proposal yet.*
2. (v) collect, arrange, organise documents systematically
finance 1. (n) money used by a company: *Where will we get the finance for this project?*
2. (v) provide money for: *The bank are going to finance the new building.*
    finances (n pl) money available: *the poor state of the company's finances*
    financial (adj) referring to finance: *financial position*
firm (n) business or partnership
fire (v inf) send away from employment, sack: *Our employment record is good in the community as we hardly ever fire anyone.*
fix (v) agree/set something: *The price was fixed at $25.*
    fix up (v) arrange
flexible (adj) can be changed
flexitime (n) (also flextime) flexible system of working in which workers can choose what time to start and finish (see also **core time**): *With the flexitime system you can choose your start and finish time.*
fluctuate (v) rise and fall rapidly: *Workers certainly don't want their pay to fluctuate wildly.*
forecast 1. (n) estimate of what will happen in the future
2. (v) predict what will happen
franchise 1. (n) licence to sell under a brand name
2. (v) give a licence to someone
fraud (n) making money by not telling the truth: *He became rich through systematic fraud.*
freelance (n & adj) person who works for him- or herself
fund 1. (n) money set aside for a special purpose: *a pension fund.*
2. (v) provide money for: *We funded the company in the early days.*
    funds (n pl) money available to spend: *We need extra funds to pay for research.*

G

gap (n) hole, unfilled space: *There's a gap in the market.*
goal (n) aim, objective
goods (n pl) products/items for sale
goodwill (n) good reputation of a business/intangible asset connected to customer base, track record etc.
graduate (n) person who has a qualification from a university
gross (adj) total, with no reductions: *Gross profit is sales minus direct costs.*
    gross margin percentage difference between sales and direct cost of sales
    gross profit profit calculated as sales less direct cost of sales

Glossary

grow (v) get bigger
   growth (n) increase in size
guarantee (n) promise that something will work well
guidelines (n pl) suggestions about how to do something: *We have read the guidelines and feel that they are acceptable.*

half-year (n) 6 months: *The first half-year was disappointing.*
head (v) be the head of, be in charge of: *The department is headed by me as personnel director.*
hire (v) take on a paid worker, employ: *Make sure you hire people with the ability to do the job.*
hold (v) own: *The chairman holds 45% of the shares.*
   holding company (n) company which acts only as a legal entity for owning shares in subsidiary companies
HRD (n) (= Human Resources Development) activities to develop the organisation's workforce
   human resources (n pl) workforce of an organisation

implement (v) put into action
   implementation (n) putting into action
incentive (n) something which motivates: *We need to offer incentives to people joining the company.*
income (n) 1. wages and salary: *Employees expect their incomes to be maintained and carry on rising.* 2. money received through operations or investment
industrial (adj) referring to manufacturing work: *Industrial marketing is very different from consumer marketing.*
   industrial action (n) strike
   industrial relations (n pl) relations between management and workers

inefficiency (n) inability to produce good results quickly: *A third problem area is the organisational stress and inefficiency usually associated with conflict.*
inflate (v) increase artificially, without reason
   inflation (n) state of rising prices
insolvent (adj) not able to pay debts: *The company will soon be insolvent.*
installation (n) activity of putting new machines into an office or a factory
instalment (n) part: *The other eight days' holiday may be taken in either one or two instalments, for example five days and three days or six days and two days.*
insure (v) protect against loss, damage, injury or death by paying a sum of money
   insurance (n) protection against loss, damage, injury or death by paying a sum of money
interest (n) a percentage of the capital paid by a borrower to a lender
interview 1. (n) meeting to decide if a person is suitable for a job: *Before closing a job interview it is useful for the interviewer to summarise the key points and issues.*
2. (v) talk to a person applying for a job
introduce (v) launch: *introduce a product on the market*
invest (v) put money into a bank, a building society or shares in order to earn interest
   investment (n) money invested
invoice 1. (n) note requesting payment
2. (v) send an invoice to someone
IT (n) (= Information Technology)
item (n) 1. an object for sale: *This item is out of stock.* 2. piece of information: *items on the balance sheet*

job (n) piece of work, work, post
   job description written statement of what the job holder actually does, how he or she does it, and under what conditions the job is performed
joint (adj) combined, shared between two or more parties

Glossary

K

key (adj) important, main: *This client is a key account.*
knowhow/know-how (n) knowledge about how something works, expertise

L

labour (n) work
   labour market (n) supply of workers available to work
   labour relations (n pl) relations between management and workers
   labour shortage (n) situation where there are not enough workers
launch 1. (v) introduce a new product on the market
2. (n) introduction of new product: *The launch was very successful.*
law (n) rules made by government: *Every employer in this country is required by law to prepare a contract of employment.*
lay-off/layoff 1. (n) action of stopping a worker's employment for a time, especially when there is little work to do
2. (v) dismiss temporarily
lead (v) 1. be the first and/or the best: *The company leads the world in design.* 2. manage/direct: *He is well-qualified to lead the team.*
legal (adj) made according to the law
lend (v) allow temporary use of
   lender (n) person who lends money
liability (n) legal obligation: *Our liability is limited.*
   liabilities (n pl) debts of a business
licence (n) [US **license**] official document which gives permission: *You need an import licence.*
   license (v) give permission
liquid (adj) easy to realise: *liquid assets*
   liquidity (n) having assets which can be converted into cash
   liquidate (v) close a company and sell its assets
   liquidation (n) process of closing a company: *The business went into liquidation.*
loan 1. (n) money which has been lent: *Loan capital must be repaid at a later date.*
2. (v) lend
lose (v) not make a profit: *We are losing money.*
   loss (n) *We suffered a loss.*
loyalty (n) sense of belonging and trusting: *customer loyalty*

M

magazine (n) regular news or special interest publication often printed on glossy paper with many photographs
mailshot (n) direct mailing related to a particular product or service
maintain (v) keep going: *We must maintain our market share.*
   maintenance (n) keeping things working: *The after-sales team work on maintenance of the products.*
major (adj) important, bigger, biggest: *The major shareholder has 35% of the shares.*
majority shareholding (n) more than 50% of the shares
make (n) brand or type of product
manage (v) control and be in charge of: *to manage a sales office*
   management (n) 1. controlling and running a business or part of a business: *management by objectives.* 2. group of people who control an organisation
   middle management (n) department managers
   senior management (n) top managers
   managerial (adj) referring to managers, at a managerial level
   manager (n) person who manages an organisation or part of it
   line manager (n) manager who is in charge of accomplishing the basic goals of the organisation
   plant manager (n) factory manager
   staff manager (n) manager who assists and advises line managers
manpower (n) total number of workers for a certain type of work or for an area
manual (adj) using the hands: *Manual employees*

Glossary

are usually represented by different unions from white-collar employees.
manufacture (v) make a product using machines
  manufacturer (n) company which produces products
margin (n) difference between sale price and cost price
  gross margin difference between manufacturing cost and sale price
  net margin difference between total cost (inc. overheads) and sale price
market (n) 1. place where a product can be sold 2. possible sales of a product
  market leader dominant company in the market
  market niche small part of specialised market
  market research examination of the possible demand for a product before it is put on the market
  market share percentage of a total market which one company or product holds
maximise (v) make as large as possible: *We must maximise profits.*
measure (n) action, step: *We are going to take measures to reduce costs.*
merge (v) join together: *The company merged with another European company.*
  merger (n) act/result of joining companies together
minimise (v) make something as small as possible: *to minimise risk*
mobility (n) ability to move
monopoly (n) market situation where one company is the only supplier of a product or service
motivate (v) give someone a reason or incentive for doing something
  motivation (n) state of being motivated: *For motivation to take place, workers must believe that effort on their part will lead to rewards.*

N

negotiate (v) discuss with another or others to reach agreement, bargain
  negotiation (n) (often plural) act of bargaining: *We are starting our annual pay negotiations next week.*

net (adj) after all deductions have been made: *net profit*
network (n) system which links different places together
niche (n) small segment of specialised market
notice (n) 1. information about something that will happen: *The workers gave the management 24 hours' notice of the strike.* 2. information that a person will leave his employment (voluntarily or not): *I've heard that three more are going to give in their notice in May.*

objective (n) target, aim
obsolete (adj) no longer used: *The old product is now obsolete.*
offer 1. (n) statement that you are willing to pay a certain amount: *We made a good offer.*
2. (v) say you are willing to pay/help
operate (v) run or work a machine/business
  operating profits profits which result from day-to-day business
opportunity (n) chance to do something: *There are opportunities and risks in this market.*
option (n) possibility, opportunity: *We have the first option to buy the property.*
order (n) request for the supply of goods: *We placed the order last week but we haven't received the goods yet*
organigram (n) diagram which shows the areas of responsibility in an organisation and the relationships between the personnel
organise (v) plan and operate something so that it works efficiently
orientation (n) direction or main area of interest
outcome (n) result: *The outcome of an interview is of great importance to the candidate.*
outlet (n) place where something can be sold: *a retail outlet*
output (n) quantity that a person or machine produces: *Incentive plans usually result in greater output per man hour.*
overdraft (n) amount of money which a person/company withdraws from a bank account and which is more than is in the account

Glossary

overdraw (v) take out more money from a bank account than is in the account
overhead (adj) day-to-day running and administrative: *Our overhead costs have increased.*
overheads (n pl) non-attributable, running costs
overtime (n) time after basic working time, normally paid at an extra rate: *However, at the end of any month you mustn't have more than 10 hours' overtime.*
overview (n) general picture or information
owe (v) have to pay money: *They owe the bank £25,000.*

P

p.a. (n) (= per annum) per year: *The starting salary will be £24,000 p.a.*
pack (v) put things into a container for sending or selling
parent company (n) company which owns more than 50% of the shares of another company
part-time (adj) working for only part of the working day: *Our part-time employees work less than 20 hours a week.*
participate (v) take part in: *The workshop will be run again next month, so you'll have an opportunity to participate.*
partnership (n) unregistered business where two or more people share risks and profits
patent (n) official registration of a new invention
pay 1. (n) money given for work or service
2. (v) give money for work or service: *pay by cheque/credit card, pay tax*
   payroll (n) 1. all employees in a company 2. the wages bill of a company
peak (n) highest point
pension (n) amount of money paid regularly after a person stops work, either because of old age or illness: *Is £140 per week, plus a pension, better than £200 per week without?*
perform (v) do well or badly: *Sometimes employees don't perform at the required standard because they don't know what the standard is.*
   performance (n) action of doing something well or badly: *The company improved their performance last year.*
personnel (n) people employed by a company: *Personnel management is directed mainly at the organisation's employees.*
pilot (n) test which will be extended if successful: *a pilot project*
   pilot study (n) test which, if succcessful, will be expanded into a full operation
pipeline (n) channel of flow: *Are there any new products in the pipeline?*
plant (n) factory
   plant manager (n) factory manager
plc PUBLIC LIMITED COMPANY
policy (n) way of doing something: *What is the company policy on discounts?*
post (n) job
potential 1. (n) person's possibilities for future development: *The organisation has an obligation to give every employee an opportunity to grow and to realise his or her full potential.*
2. (adj) possible future
power (n) strength
   purchasing power discounts that can be obtained by buying in large quantities
price (n) money paid for a product
   market price price which people are willing to pay
   retail price price paid by final customer
product (n) thing which is made/manufactured
   production (n) what is produced by a company
   productive (adj) producing well or much: *There is also a general feeling that employees who are well looked after by the employer will be more productive.*
   productivity (n) measurement of output per worker
profit (n) money gained from doing business
   operating profit profits from normal trading of a company
   profit and loss account [US: **income statement**] accounts showing income and expenditure
   profitability (n) ability to make a profit
   profitable (adj) which makes a profit
progress (n) forward movement
project (n) plan

Glossary

promote (v) 1. give someone a better job: *Up till now we've promoted the analyst/programmers to junior project leaders.* 2. advertise
   promotion (n) 1. act of giving someone a better job
2. all means of communicating a message about a product or service
proposal (n) suggestion
prospect (n) possibility for the future
prospectus (n) 1. sales document which tries to convince the customer, usually using a serious approach
2. document issued by a company offering shares for sale
prototype (n) first model of a new product
public (adj) referring to people in general
   public sector nationalised industries
publicity (n) the process of attracting the attention of the general public to products or services
punctual (adj) on time
   punctuality (n) being on time
purchase 1. (n) something which has been bought: *It will be cheaper to make a quantity purchase.*
2. (v) buy
   purchaser (n) person who buys for a company

Q

qualify (v) have the right education and background
   qualified (adj) with the right education and experience: *If we want to recruit suitably qualified staff, we mustn't have a further fall in pay.*
   qualification/s (n) education, ability or experience: *He plans to go back to college to get a management qualification.*
quality (n) the value/worth of a product/service
   quality control checking that the quality is high enough
quarterly (adj/adv) happening four times a year, every 3 months: *Our quarterly results were excellent.*
questionnaire (n) form consisting of a number of questions

quote 1. (v) estimate the value/cost: *Could you quote for the contract in dollars?*
2. (n) estimate
   quotation (n) 1. estimate of cost 2. listing of the price of a share on the Stock Exchange

R

R & D RESEARCH AND DEVELOPMENT
raise 1. (n) US increase in salary: *She asked for a raise.*
2. (v) 1. increase: *We raised the dividend by 5%.* 2. obtain: *We are trying to raise $50,000 on the money market.* 3. bring up in discussion: *We raised the question of prices at the board meeting.*
range (n) series of products which the customer can choose from
rank 1. (n) position in a company or list
2. (v) classify in order of importance: *The company is ranked 6th in the world.*
rate (n) money charged for a certain time or at a certain percentage
   fixed rate charge which cannot be changed
ratio (n) proportion of something compared to another thing: *Our liquidity ratio is not healthy (current assets to current liabilities).*
rationalise (v) make more efficient, streamline
   rationalisation (n) the activity of making something more efficient
raw (adj) in its original, unprocessed state
   raw materials substances used as a base for manufacturing
receive (v) get
   receipt (n) piece of paper showing that money has been paid or something received: *a receipt for items purchased*
   receiver (n) government official appointed to run a company in serious financial difficulty
recover (v) get better after a downturn: *The stock market has not recovered since the big fall.*
   recovery (n) improvement, getting back to the previous (better) position
recruit (v) take on a new person: *Our trade union has recruited a number of new members this year.*
   recruitment (n) process of taking on new

Glossary

people: *Ads remain a good source of management recruitment.*
red (n) **in the red** showing a loss: *My bank account is always in the red.*
reduce (v) make smaller: *We need to reduce our prices.*
   reduction (n) the state of being smaller, lowering
redundant (adj) having lost one's job
   redundancy (n) state of having lost one's job
reference (n) written report on someone's personality and/or ability, often written by a previous employer
refund 1. (n) money paid back
2. (v) pay back money: *The money will be refunded if the goods are faulty.*
region (n) area
reject 1. (n) something that is not accepted
2. (v) not accept
reliability (n) quality of something which can be trusted
remuneration (n) pay
rent 1. (n) money paid to use an office/property for a period of time
2. (v) pay money for the use of offices etc.
rep (n) abbreviation for representative
report to (v) be under (someone): *Then there are four managers who report to me.*
represent (v) work on behalf of: *He represented Rossomon at the conference.*
   representative (n) salesperson
reputation (n) opinion held by others: *High pay rates succeed in getting an organisation the reputation of being a good employer.*
require (v) need
   requirement (n) what is needed: *Then we must consider the organisation's requirements.*
research (n) investigation to find information
resign (v) give up one's job
   resignation (n) the act of giving up one's job
respond (v) reply
   response (n) answer to a question, reaction to a product or service
result/s (n) profit or loss at the end of an accounting period: *We announced some good results for last year.*

retail 1. (n) sale of goods to the end customer
2. (v) sell goods direct to customers
   retailer (n) person who sells goods direct
retire (v) stop working because of old age or illness
   retirement (n) time when one stops working because of old age or illness: *As retirement approaches, employees start to think of alternatives to work.*
return (n) profit from an investment: *What sort of return can we expect?*
   return on investment ROI
revenue (n) income received
review 1. (v) look at in general: *In the future we intend to review performance standards at least twice a year.*
2. (n) look, check: *an annual review*
reward 1. (n) something given for good work: *The supervisor's praise may be enough of a reward to keep productivity up.*
2. (v) give something for good work: *Your incentive plan should therefore reward employees in direct proportion to their increased productivity.*
risk (n) chance of success or failure: *take a risk*
   risky (adj) *That's a risky venture.*
rival 1. (n) competitor
2. (adj) competing
ROI RETURN ON INVESTMENT
roughly (adv) approximately
round up/down (v) increase/decrease to a round number
royalty (n) money paid to an inventor/creator/writer by the licensee or publisher
run (v) manage, organise: *He runs two businesses.*
   running (adj) 1. operating: *running costs*
2. continuing: *We keep a running total from day to day.* 3. continuously: *We have made a loss for 2 years running.*

S

sack 1. (v) dismiss
2. (n) termination of employment: *He was given the sack.*
salary (n) pay, usually expressed as an annual sum and paid monthly: *The payroll consists of the wages and salaries paid to employees.*

Glossary

save (v) keep, not spend money
   savings (n pl) money saved
scale (n) system for measuring, divided into levels: *We can evaluate performance on a scale from 1 to 5.*
seasonal (adj) which only happens in certain seasons: *Ice-cream sales are very seasonal.*
section (n) part of a department: *The personnel department is divided into 5 sections, each dealing with a specialist area.*
sector (n) part of the economy or industry: *The hi-tech sector is growing fast.*
segment 1. (n) section of the market
2. (v) divide a market into different parts
select (v) choose
   selection (n) act of choosing
semi-skilled (adj) with some training: *semi-skilled workers*
service (n) 1. work of dealing with customers: *The service is excellent – we never have to wait.*
2. maintaining a machine in good working order: *The photocopier is due for a service.*
   services (n pl) benefits which do not involve production such as training, transportation
settle (v) agree on a solution to a problem
set up (v) establish
share (n) 1. **market share**: percentage of a market held by a company or a product
2. small part of a company's capital
   shareholder (n) person who owns shares in a company
shift (n) part of the working day in a factory: *You need to decide some time before next Monday if you want to work the early shift or the late shift.*
sick (adj) ill
   sick pay (n) money paid during absence from work through illness: *Younger workers are more interested in high direct earnings at the expense of indirect benefits, like pensions and sick pay.*
   sickness (n) illness
skill (n) ability
   skilled employee (n) worker who has had full training: *Skilled employees are sometimes represented by a different union from the semi-skilled and unskilled.*

slump (n) rapid decrease: *a slump in sales*
software (n) programs for a computer system
solvent (adj) having enough money to pay debts
specifications (n pl) size
split (v) divide
sponsor (n) person or company paying for an event (sports, culture etc.)
staff (n) people employed by a company
steadily (adv) in a regular or continuous way
stock (n) 1. quantity of goods for sale – inventories
2. stocks and shares – shares in ordinary companies – stock often refers to fixed interest securities (loan stock) [US **bonds**]
   stockbroker (n) person who buys and sells shares for clients
   stock exchange (n) market in which securities are traded
storage (n) keeping in store
strategy (n) future action to achieve objectives
   strategic (adj) referring to a plan of action
stress (n) worry caused by difficulties: *A second drawback of conflict is the emotional stress for the participants.*
strike (n) work stoppage organised by workers or trade union *Everyone in that section is on strike.*
structure (n) organisation
subcontract (v) arrange with another company to do some work
subordinate 1. (n) person below another in the company hierarchy
2. (adj) lower: *subordinate position*
subscribe (v) 1. pay in advance for a number of issues of a publication 2. apply for shares: *subscribe to a new share issue*
   subscription (n) 1. money paid in advance for a new publication 2. the act of subscribing to a new share issue
subsidiary (n) company which is at least 51% owned by a parent company
subsidise (v) help or support financially: *The Government subsidises new investment in depressed areas.*
   subsidy (n) money given to support unprofitable enterprises
summarise (v) explain in short

Glossary

superior (n) person above another in the company hierarchy
supervisor (n) person who is in charge of others: *A supervisor looks after the workers in a section.*
supply 1. (n) provision: *We are subject to the laws of supply and demand.*
2. (v) provide something
    supplier (n) person or company supplying goods or services
support (v) help
survey (n) investigation: *Recent surveys have shown that productivity is increasing.*

T

takeover (n) buying an existing business: *We are fighting a takeover bid.*
target 1. (n) aim: *Our sales targets are high.*
2. (v) aim at: *We have targeted the 30-45 age group.*
task (n) job or part of a job: *Employees must also perceive they can actually do the tasks required.*
tax 1. (n) money charged by the government or an official body to pay for services
2. (v) make somebody pay tax
    income tax tax on personal income
    value added tax (VAT) tax on goods and services
temporary (adj) only for a short or limited time
territory (n) sales or business area
track record (n) experience and results of a company or person over a number of years: *His track record speaks for itself.*
trade 1. (n) business of buying and selling: *We depend on overseas trade.*
2. (v) buy and sell: *He trades in shares.*
    trading profit gross income exceeding total costs
trademark (n) registered name or design of a company which cannot be used by another company
trade union (n) group of workers organised together in order to bargain with management about terms and conditions of employment: *Trade union recognition is widespread in Britain, although there has been a drop of over two million members since 1980.*
train (v) teach or learn

trainee (n) person who is learning: *The trainee will work directly with the person he or she is to replace.*
transfer 1. (n) movement of something to another place: *We credited your account by bank transfer.*
2. (v) move something from one place to another: *We transferred our money to the Cayman Islands.*
transparency (n) clear plastic material used on an overhead projector to show information
trend (n) general development in a market/business: *There is a downward trend in inflation.*
turnover (n) 1. total amount of sales: *Our turnover in 1991 was 25% up on 1990.* 2. speed at which staff or stock change
    staff turnover speed at which staff changes

U

unemployment (n) state of being without a job
    unemployment benefit (n) money paid by the state to people without jobs
unit (n) single item: *The unit cost goes down as production increases.*
update (v) bring up to date
up-to-date (adj/adv) current, modern
upgrade (v) improve
upturn (n) movement upwards: *There has been a marked upturn in sales.*

V

vacancy (n) job which needs to be filled
    vacant (adj) open (of a job): *One of the positions is vacant at present.*
value 1. (n) amount something is worth
2. (v) estimate how much something is worth
variable (n) factor which will change results: *There are too many variables to take into account.*
variation (n) amount by which something changes: *Seasonal variations account for much of the drop in sales.*
variety (n) range of things: *The wholesaler stocks a variety of products.*
    vary (v) differ, change: *The margin varies depending on raw material costs.*

Glossary

VAT VALUE ADDED TAX
viable (adj) workable, able to be profitable: *This project is not viable.*
vocation (n) type of work that a person has an ability or desire for

W

wage (n) weekly pay: *The wage rise last year was 7.5%.*
warehouse (n) building where goods are stored
wealth (n) 1. large amount of money owned by someone 2. resources of a country
   wealthy (adj) rich
welfare (n) system of looking after employees: *Health and safety are aspects of employee welfare.*

white-collar (adj) relating to office workers: *White-collar workers represent a significant part of the organisation.*
wholesale (n, adj & adv) buying goods from a manufacturer and selling on to retailers
   wholesaler (n) person/company who buys from manufacturers and sells to retailers
withdraw (v) take away
work (n) job(s), employment
   working conditions (n pl) general physical state of the place where people work, including things like noise level, hazardous conditions, or heat
write off (v) cancel/remove a debt from the accounts: *The debt has been written off.*
   write-off (n) loss/cancellation of a bad debt

Appendix

IRREGULAR VERBS

Present Simple/ infinitive	Past Simple	Past participle
be	was/were	been
beat	beat	beaten
become	became	become
begin	began	begun
break	broke	broken
bring	brought	brought
build	built	built
buy	bought	bought
catch	caught	caught
choose	chose	chosen
come	came	come
cost	cost	cost
cut	cut	cut
do	did	done
draw	drew	drawn
drink	drank	drunk
drive	drove	driven
eat	ate	eaten
fall	fell	fallen
feel	felt	felt
fight	fought	fought
find	found	found
fly	flew	flown
forget	forgot	forgotten
get	got	got *(British)*
get	got	gotten *(American)*
give	gave	given
go	went	gone/been
grow	grew	grown
have	had	had
hear	heard	heard
hide	hid	hidden
hit	hit	hit
hold	held	held
keep	kept	kept
know	knew	known
lay	laid	laid
lead	led	led
leave	left	left
lend	lent	lent
let	let	let

Present Simple/ infinitive	Past Simple	Past participle
lie	lay	lain
lose	lost	lost
make	made	made
mean	meant	meant
meet	met	met
pay	paid	paid
put	put	put
read	read	read
ride	rode	ridden
rise	rose	risen
run	ran	run
say	said	said
see	saw	seen
sell	sold	sold
send	sent	sent
set	set	set
shine	shone	shone
shoot	shot	shot
show	showed	shown
shut	shut	shut
sing	sang	sung
sink	sank	sunk
sit	sat	sat
sleep	slept	slept
speak	spoke	spoken
spend	spent	spent
split	split	split
stand	stood	stood
steal	stole	stolen
strike	struck	struck
swim	swam	swum
take	took	taken
teach	taught	taught
tell	told	told
think	thought	thought
throw	threw	thrown
understand	understood	understood
wake	woke	woken
wear	wore	worn
win	won	won
write	wrote	written